SUNČANA LAKETA

CITIES OF BANAL WARFARE

Affective Geographies in Violent Times

First published in Great Britain in 2025 by

Bristol University Press
University of Bristol
1–9 Old Park Hill
Bristol
BS2 8BB
UK
t: +44 (0)117 374 6645
e: bup-info@bristol.ac.uk

Details of international sales and distribution partners are available at
bristoluniversitypress.co.uk

© Sunčana Laketa 2025

The digital PDF and ePub versions of this title are available open access and
distributed under the terms of the Creative Commons Attribution-NonCommercial-
NoDerivatives 4.0 International licence (https://creativecommons.org/licenses/
by-nc-nd/4.0/) which permits reproduction and distribution for non-commercial
use without further permission provided the original work is attributed.

Open access book funded by the Swiss National Science Foundation.

British Library Cataloguing in Publication Data
A catalogue record for this book is available from the British Library

ISBN 978-1-5292-5001-5 paperback
ISBN 978-1-5292-4293-5 ePub
ISBN 978-1-5292-4294-2 OA ePdf

The right of Sunčana Laketa to be identified as author of this work has been
asserted by her in accordance with the Copyright, Designs and Patents Act 1988.

All rights reserved: no part of this publication may be reproduced, stored in
a retrieval system, or transmitted in any form or by any means, electronic,
mechanical, photocopying, recording, or otherwise without the prior permission
of Bristol University Press.

Every reasonable effort has been made to obtain permission to reproduce
copyrighted material. If, however, anyone knows of an oversight, please contact
the publisher.

The statements and opinions contained within this publication are solely those of
the author and not of the University of Bristol or Bristol University Press. The
University of Bristol and Bristol University Press disclaim responsibility for any
injury to persons or property resulting from any material
published in this publication.

Bristol University Press works to counter discrimination on
grounds of gender, race, disability, age and sexuality.

Cover design: blu inc
Front cover image: Lucie Benk instagram.com/luciebenk

Contents

List of Figures		iv
Acknowledgements		v
Author's Note		vii
Prologue: War Spills Over		viii
one	Reversing the Gaze, Rethinking Urban Conflict	1
two	Urban Warfare: From State of Emergency to Lockdown	23
three	Everyday Urban Landscapes as Battlescapes	38
four	Affective Atmospheres "on the Front Line"	61
five	Affective Unsettling of Urban Warfare	84
Conclusion: The Urbicidal Geographies of Cities of Banal Warfare		101
Notes		105
References		107
Index		125

List of Figures

3.1	Brussels metro, June 2016	39
3.2	Bollards in Brussels, September 2019	48
3.3	Excerpt from *Guide à l'intégration de dispositifs de sécurité dans l'espace public: Région de Bruxelles-Capitale* (2018)	49
4.1	The Canal area of Brussels on the border of Molenbeek, July 2023	72
4.2	Masks and security infrastructure on the square at the Place de la République, August 2020	78

Acknowledgements

This book is the result of a project generously funded by the Swiss National Science Foundation through the Ambizione grant. I am particularly grateful for their support, which extended to the open access fund, enabling this book to be freely available online.

I am deeply indebted to all the individuals and institutions who participated in and supported this project. My thanks go to the institutions and organizations in Paris and Brussels that welcomed the project, offering invaluable insights into their daily work. I am equally grateful to the residents of these cities who joined in walkalongs, shared their perspectives, and collaborated in exploring the sense of place through experimental approaches.

Special thanks are due to the project's research assistants, whose contributions were indispensable at various stages—from conducting research to identifying and contacting interview partners, and facilitating the walkalongs in both cities. I extend my gratitude to Délia Rémy, Flora Hergon, Nadia El Hakim, Gilad Dadon, and Chantal Vanoeteren.

I would also like to acknowledge my colleagues at the University of Neuchâtel, Institute of Geography, which served as my academic home throughout the project. My heartfelt thanks go to my English language editor for their flexibility and continuous feedback, as well as to the team at Bristol University Press for their support during the publication process.

The manuscript benefited from early feedback provided by colleagues during its draft stages. It was presented at the workshop "Interrogating the Geopolitical: Ethnographic Engagements" at Utrecht University, and the workshop "Situational Awareness: Sensing Insecurity and Coming Catastrophes" at Hamburg University. I am grateful to the organizers and participants of these workshops for their constructive comments and insights.

I also want to thank Katherine Sammler and Flora Hergon for a detailed reading and invaluable feedback on the final manuscript, as well as to Simone Tulumello for the not-so-anonymous peer review of the book. Moreover, a special note of appreciation goes to Katherine Sammler for her creative input, energy, and enthusiasm during my time in Paris and Brussels.

Finally, I would like to express my gratitude to Lucie Benk for her creative and beautiful depictions of the stories within this book, which she skillfully compiled into a comic book.

To everyone who contributed to the project in ways big and small, thank you for your support, collaboration, and inspiration.

Author's Note

A comic book was developed, on the basis of the results of this study, in collaboration with Lucie Benk. Benk's work vividly captures the emotional and affective dimensions of the urban landscapes explored in this study—an aspect often difficult to convey through words alone.

The comic in French and English language is freely available for download here: https://doi.org/10.5281/zenodo.14220235

Prologue: War Spills Over

I am on a crowded TGV train going from Zurich to Paris, chatting to a person sitting opposite me, a Swiss businessman headed to Paris for meetings. I'm telling him about my research in Paris and Brussels, how I'm interested in the repercussions of the ostensible "terrorist" violence in the two cities, a discussion I've had numerous times on this same route. He listens half-attentively and then remarks offhand: "Ah, wars, those used to be things happening somewhere else, far away, but look at what we have here today. War is spilling over here as well!" He seems annoyed by, rather than particularly afraid of, this troubling appearance of "war" happening "here," as if this realization does not fit neatly within his imagined geographies of what happens where. In fact, what the man does not see, or ask about, is that I come from those places where wars seem to be almost a natural occurrence.

Conventionally described using the trope of the powder keg and phrases like "ethnic hatred" and "senseless violence," the Balkans, especially Bosnia and Herzegovina, where I grew up, have for decades and even centuries been the convenient placeholders for war. My fellow traveler on the Zurich–Paris train, of course, assumes with confidence that I share his worldview and does not question my own standing on this issue of war. While I'm taken aback by his comments, I do not challenge him, and he continues to rant about how "things have changed, and nobody is safe anymore." However, despite his troubling talk, his comments that day have in various ways stuck to, followed, and shaped the work of this book, reverberating throughout my research into the violence that has shaken the cities of Paris and Brussels.

The book engages with the question of what happens when "war spills over." What kind of possibilities are opened when the notion of warfare cannot be so easily contained, dismissed, or relegated as something happening "over there"? And, importantly, what kind of wars are we talking about when we discuss places such as Paris or Brussels? I begin with this notion of "war spilling over" to throw into question the common perception of a comfortable distance in relation to war, unlike my fellow train traveler, whose comments aimed to reestablish conventional boundaries between here and there. *Cities of Banal Warfare* is a deliberate attempt to engage with the spillover and harness its possibilities in order to explore its subversive and perhaps emancipatory potential. For sure, wars have been spilling over to western metropolises for decades, not least with refugees and displaced people fleeing armed conflict in search of safety. Moreover, the idea that "nobody is safe anymore" elides the fact that many people in Paris and Brussels, most notably residents of the disadvantaged neighborhoods in each city, have long been subjected to deadly violence on a regular basis. So, instead of bracketing the notion of warfare and relegating it to uncivilized, exotic elsewheres, I begin by putting in relation war-torn global urban peripheries with metropolitan centers. Starting from this relational urban geography, the book considers war not as a delimited violent event or a temporal suspension of "peaceful" social norms, but as a condition of life that continues to shape how cities are imagined, how they look, and how they feel. What follows is an exploration of the everyday material, emotional, and affective conditions of warfare that are enacted, by various actors, in the cities of Paris and Brussels, centering predominantly, but not exclusively, on the practices and discourses of "anti-terrorism."

The book asks: How does the notion of warfare animate the everyday geographies of the city? And with what effects?

ONE

Reversing the Gaze, Rethinking Urban Conflict

Cities nowadays are at the epicenter of international conflict. Consider the current wars in Ukraine and Gaza and the devastating impacts this violence is having on these cities and their urban residents. There, we are witnessing the ravaging effects of contemporary urban warfare, from the destruction of vital infrastructure so necessary in providing water, food, and sanitation to the extensive harm to residents themselves, including death and physical harm as well as psychological harm, suffering, and trauma. Growing populations of displaced individuals and families, as people flee conflicts in search of safety, are another tragic outcome of the intensification of warfare in urban areas. In recent decades, numerous cities have turned into battlegrounds; take, for instance, the siege of Sarajevo or the destruction of places such as Grozny, Fallujah, Aleppo, and Raqqa. These and many other cities across the so-called global south and global east have been rendered terrains of warfare as part of organized military actions that target residents and urban areas as a unique strategy of war.

The intensified urban warfare we are witnessing throughout global urban peripheries is, however, complexly intertangled with the metropolises of the global north. While warfare appears to be outsourced to distant urban frontiers, it has an unacknowledged hidden presence in the metropolitan centers. Cities in conflict zones are often synonymous with deathscapes—geographies where violence and death are normalized, allowing the violence of war to be viewed as endemic to those regions. While the urban frontiers are overtly marked by violence, the metropolitan centers quietly sustain and perpetuate it. These cities, while not bombarded by drones or riddled with gunfire, are integral to the mechanisms of war, housing the infrastructure, technologies, and discourses that support and sustain global conflicts. The main aim of the book is to interrogate the sites and relations that constitute urban warfare in the metropolises of the global north, places often considered to be at the center of European ideas of civilization and modernity. The purpose is not to discredit the harm and suffering of people occupying the global urban peripheries, but to reposition notions of warfare away from their conventional placeholders and to reverse the gaze on urban warfare. I do this by drawing on theories and knowledge developed from and with war-torn cities to understand how warfare is deeply entangled with mundane urban life. The book seeks to not only push the boundaries of what is considered urban warfare, but also, more importantly, interrogate the normalization of mechanisms of power that produce warfare as a lifeworld and an embodied system of meaning across different geographies.

In addressing processes of normalization of warfare, the book is grounded in the exploration of everyday urban spaces and seemingly mundane experiences in the city. The aim is to shed light on how war as a condition is sutured into the ebb and flow of everyday life. To make sense of the everyday wars within cities of the global north, the book develops the notion of "banal warfare." Here, the idea of permanent urban warfare, and the vision of urban futures ridden with conflict, terrorist attacks, diseases, and population migrations, is rendered normal, even banal. The banal warfare conceptualization allows the questioning of military logics of control and defense that infuse everyday urban life to the point of becoming invisible or taken for granted. Departing from this idea, the book focuses on the places, social orders, experiences and subjectivities generated in relation to the banality of urban warfare.

The chapters center on the cities of Paris and Brussels to explore the way wars and urban places are mutually co-constituted, asking how wars are shaping cities as well as how cities are shaping warfare. These two cities, historically formed as colonial centers, continue to embody the paradox of being peaceful European capitals while playing pivotal roles in contemporary military and neocolonial engagements. As part of French and Belgian military superpowers, these cities are complexly intertangled with conflicts far beyond their borders. France, with its legacy of colonial rule in Africa and the Middle East, remains actively involved in military interventions, such as in Mali and Syria, often under the guise of counterterrorism or humanitarianism. Similarly, Belgium's involvement in North Atlantic Treaty Organization (known as NATO) and European Union (EU) military actions reflects a continuation of its imperial mindset, influencing geopolitical dynamics in regions like Central Africa. Despite this, Paris and Brussels are not conventionally viewed as cities at war; they are instead seen as peaceful metropolises, since World War II at least. At the same time, these cities' roles as colonial centers have deeply shaped their social and urban landscapes, fostering environments marked by xenophobic and violent migrant regimes. Immigrants, particularly those from former colonies, often face systemic discrimination, marginalization, and police violence, reflecting the unresolved legacies of colonialism.

As a way to challenge this paradox, I begin by viewing the two cities through a relational prism that underscores how banal warfare translates onto, and emerges through, urban public space. The particular focus is on the implementation of urban security measures: the state of emergency in Paris and the lockdown in Brussels. Drawing from diverse methodologies, the book develops two interrelated arguments. On the one hand, it argues that the emerging geographies of everyday war work to constitute subjects and objects of security, danger, and threat. And on the other hand, it argues that these geographies further normalize militarism and conflict in urban contexts typically regarded as "non-war" in ways that link these spaces to others more conventionally considered as (post)war cities and sites.

Urbicidal geographies and military urbanism

To understand how conditions of war infuse the everyday urban geographies of Paris and Brussels, I take as a point of departure the wars in the Yugoslav republics and cities during the 1990s and the concept of "urbicide" that those wars gave prominence to. Urbicide refers to a targeted destruction of urban places as a strategy of war, and in the early 1990s many cities across the Balkan region were subjected to utter destruction and annihilation. The "killing of cities" in the Balkans involved the infamous destruction of the Old Bridge and several other public places in Mostar as well as public places in numerous other cities in the region, from Vukovar to Mitrovica. It was the Mostar Architects Association, including the architect and urbanist Bogdan Bogdanović, that drew attention to these urbicidal practices and denounced the destruction of the urban built environment that was happening alongside, and related to, the tragic human loss (Makaš, 2007). Their raising of the subject of urbicide also sought to contest the powerful orientalist imaginaries of warfare in the Balkans that were popular in western media and academic discourses at the time. The widespread western political discourses saw these forms of warfare as irrational, barbaric, and senseless acts of destruction and constructed an imaginative geography of the Balkans as a place of primordial violence, an essentialist deathscape (Kaplan, 1993; Cohen, 1995; see also Bakić-Hayden, 1995; Bjelić and Savić, 2002). In this discourse, sometimes referred to as "Balkanism" (an analogy based on Edward Said's notion of orientalism; see Said, 1979), the Balkans played a crucial role in the west's "progressive" self-image of Enlightenment Europe and the "civilized" west. The representations of armed conflict in the Balkans as primitive and savage wars were positioned as opposites to the western emphasis on strategic interests, rational tactics, and ethical conduct in situations of war. Thus, the orientalist view on warfare in the cities in the Balkans repudiated the idea of the urban destruction as a purposeful military strategy enacted to achieve certain political goals. Rather, by portraying the violence as barbaric, the orientalist depictions and narratives designated the urban warfare in the Balkans as acts of destruction defying rational explanation, acts that are in stark contrast to European ideas of civilization. In this way, war and violence were represented as natural features of the place and the Balkan people rather than as serving a particular political purpose.

Bogdanović and others showed the urbicidal violence was not senseless but a deliberate and conscious means of accomplishing a political goal. They argued urbicide worked to enable, entrench, and exacerbate the political project of creating ethno-nationally homogenous polity and territoriality in the Balkans. It did so by annihilating the very material (infra)structures that promoted social encounters as the very basis of the formation of heterogenous communities. Systematic urbicidal place annihilation was, and continues to be, essential in constructing different geographies of exclusion and sustaining ethno-national power. Coward (2009) adds that the destruction of urban places across the Balkans shows the capacity of the urban built environment to enable the condition of heterogeneity. Here, the urban center facilitates the creation of communities based on shared spatialities and engagements with the commons in ways that undermine the military logics of division and the political aim of creating exclusionary identities. Urbicide thus, as part of a particular political project, annihilates the city's social and emotional sense of place as a site of encounter.

In the decade after the wars in the Balkans, the concept of urbicide was taken up within Anglo-American debates emerging in the wake of the "global war on terror," following the destruction of the World Trade Center in New York City.

At the time, scholars, as well as military actors, started noting the urban character of contemporary warfare, arguing wars were becoming increasingly urbanized (Kaldor, 1999). Western military studies began to identify urban warfare as one of the main challenges to western military might in late modern warfare. Gradually, military labels and related acronyms, such as "urban operations," or "UO," and "military operations on urban terrain," or "MOUT," were put in place to account for the supposedly changing nature of warfare in the so-called "new global order." The evolving military strategy included, among other things, the building of mock Arab cities in the deserts of Israel and the US for military training purposes (Graham, 2011).

While some scholars, such as Mary Kaldor (1999), argue that contemporary wars represent a significant departure from previous forms, emphasizing the uniqueness of "new wars" characterized by decentralized, irregular combat and the targeting of civilians, others, such as Sara Fregonese (2019), caution against viewing cities at war as a completely novel phenomenon, instead tracing a long genealogy of urban warfare throughout history. Regardless of whether these conflicts are genuinely "new," these scholarly debates and evolving military doctrines are performative in nature—they do not merely describe urban warfare but actively contribute to its conceptualization and practice. By framing the city as a distinct and strategic terrain of conflict, these discourses have effectively brought the notion of urban warfare into being, shaping how cities are perceived and engaged with in an increasingly urbanized world. This performative dimension has solidified the city's role as a critical battlefield, influencing both the conduct of war and the broader understanding of the relationship between urban spaces and conflict (Graham, 2008; Yacobi, 2009; Fregonese, 2012).

Moreover, with renewed attention to urbicide, scholars have documented a wide range of "killing of the city" that was occurring within the cities of the global south, from Palestine and Israel to Iraq, Afghanistan, and others (Yiftachel, 1998; Gregory, 2004; Kipfer and Goonewardena, 2007; Weizman, 2007; Ramadan, 2009; Abujidi, 2014; Fregonese, 2019). These extreme cases of urban warfare provide insights into the specific political objectives and strategies that motivate different forms of the killing of the city. They show that with global interconnectivity and increased urbanization, targeting urban infrastructures produces wide-ranging societal and political effects. In other words, military forces purposefully demolish extensive urban infrastructures since they are a part of the intricate infrastructural networks that are essential to modern society.

The idea of a global interconnectivity is further underscored in the concept of "military urbanism." The concept has been developed to account for the complex interconnections between war-torn cities and the metropolises of the global north, aiming to designate a potentially novel way of organizing and imagining the city through a military lens. For Stephen Graham (2011), military urbanism refers to the deployment of (new) military tactics, infrastructure, and equipment as well as the implementation of the military logics of control and defense in cities across the global south and north. Graham argues that the intensified urban warfare affecting global urban peripheries is intertangled with increased securitization. Drawing examples predominantly from cities in the UK and the US, Graham shows how high-tech surveillance systems, such as the use of drones for policing the city, the deployment of data mining, and the use of biometric surveillance techniques, are simultaneously implemented in global urban peripheries and western metropolitan centers. In doing so, a transnational space of urban warfare and militarism is being forged where the developments in one city converge with the military power in another city. The processes of military urbanism are initiated not only by traditional state actors, but increasingly by private and corporate actors that form part of the burgeoning transnational security markets. This political economy of warfare is further sustained through forms of cultural power that suffuse everyday urban life in the metropolises of the global north, from the design of war video games to the development of "gated communities." This cultural landscape is, for Graham, crucial in further normalizing and legitimizing militarism and political violence in everyday urban environments.

The processes of military urbanism can be understood as an example of the so-called "boomerang effect," signifying the way practices, techniques, and narratives deployed in the colonies are being imported back to the center. For example, Martinican poet and writer Aimé Césaire (2014/1950) addresses the "boomerang effect" in relation to the Holocaust in Europe during World War II, arguing that the racial logic of genocidal violence was initially directed at the European colonies and then deployed back to the colonial centers in the form of the Holocaust. In contemporary military urbanism, the boomerang effect accounts for the process in which the (former) colonies can be understood as testing grounds, or laboratories, for implementing military techniques, concepts, and technologies, which are then imported to govern the racialized urban population of the center. The colonial underpinnings of state power, and of police work (Neocleous, 2014; Rigouste, 2021), are thus essential in understanding the linkages and convergences between war-torn cities and places that are not conventionally considered as cities at war, a topic further addressed in the following section.

Decolonial urbanism: theorizing with war-torn cities

The notion of military urbanism, and the boomerang effect, helped to rethink and contest the Eurocentric notion of warfare as something that happens *over there*, in far away and foreign places that are fundamentally different to Western notions of urban modernity. With this book, I want to take a step further to reclaim urban peripheries as constitutive of urban knowledge production. In other words, I want to strengthen the commitments to decolonial urbanism by further reversing the gaze on urban warfare. I do this by sourcing the theory from and with global urban peripheries, in an example of what Edward Said (1994/1983) calls "travelling theory." While, traditionally, urban theories originate in the west and then travel to become implemented in the cities of the global south and east, this book disrupts and shifts the conventional trajectories of diffusion and translation. It engages by theorizing *with*, rather than about, the war-torn cities to consider the way these places are generative of new knowledge and approaches that reformulate our theories, concepts, and methodologies.

For many people occupying global urban peripheries, wars and armed conflict are conditions they have long been living with. Wars, as such, need to be understood as not only destructive but also generative forces. Wars create social, material, and cultural relations that become inscribed in the landscape and the collective sense of place. Having grown up in Bosnia and Herzegovina, I have learned how wars shape places, social relations, and subjectivities long after the dramatic violence. Wars shape the narrative structures of our lives and family histories, transmitted over generations. Different wars become enduring forces that frame the contours of our collective lifeworlds. The experience of living in the Balkans during the wars in the 1990s has, among other things, defined my embodied understanding of the pervasiveness of militarist discourses and their devastating effect on the day-to-day lives of families and communities. The theory developed to understand the banality of urban warfare references on these experiences and my own situatedness as a source of embodied meaning-making. This emerging theoretical framework further references knowledges developed with postwar cities in the Balkans, and other global urban peripheries, to challenge conventional, colonial, and Eurocentric accounts of warfare. As Munira Khayyat writes: "We must decolonize our epistemic terrain, adjust our political stakes, source our theory and ground our ethnography and other representational genres in worlds and words that do not comfortably inhabit hegemonic imperial geographies and tropes" (2022: 15).

Academic knowledge construction operates along an often-undisclosed colonial logic. To begin with, theorizations of urban dynamics have historically been deeply rooted in the experiences of Euro-American contexts (Roy, 2009). Academic scholarship on urban issues has traditionally depended on Eurocentric notions of urbanity, evaluating other cities in comparison to the European urban prototype (Robinson, 2022). Western urban theories thus frame and structure the ways of knowing the cities in the global south and east (Parnell and Oldfield, 2014; Roy, 2016; Bhan, 2019; Yiftachel, 2020; Chadwick, 2021; Ren, 2022; Ortiz, 2023). Urban theories themselves are established within the matrix of coloniality and imperialism where non-western regions feature as testing grounds for western theories, similar to how military doctrine uses colonial peripheries as laboratories for testing military technologies. This is a form of epistemic coloniality (Roy, 2016) whose structures and effects extend way beyond urban theory, driving scholarly and activist efforts to reexamine imbalances of power that are inherent in the process of knowledge construction (Boatca, 2006; Blagojević, 2009; Cusicanqui, 2012; Kušić et al, 2019).

The Eurocentric theories on cities at war, specifically those theories developed after World War II, often rest on the construction of binaries between modern, civilized, and peaceful western metropolises and savage global urban peripheries, mired in violence. These theories and depictions use the strategy of spatial displacement to disavow violence from the metropole, but also, importantly, to sustain and naturalize colonial violence in global urban peripheries. Efforts to decolonize knowledge production are thus also essential for opposing the military logics of urban warfare that operate through erasure and marginalization of the very voices that endure and resist geopolitical violence. In theorizing with war-torn cities, "the political and intellectual task is to recognize (decolonize, unsavage) war as a process integral to the 'normal' workings of capitalism and the nation-state" (Khayyat, 2022: 14). In other words, I reference the theoretical body of knowledge generated with war-torn cities to reformulate the dominant understanding of what urban warfare is and where it takes place. In reversing the gaze on urban warfare, I aim to explore and find new avenues to understand contemporary military urbanism in Paris and Brussels as the metropolises of the global north.

In theorizing with war-torn cities, urban warfare is not understood as a time-delimited event confined to the space of the armed battleground, but rather it needs to be regarded as having a protracted and processual quality that extends into the intimate spaces of the everyday. In other words, in so-called post-conflict cities, or what the military doctrine calls places of "low-intensity warfare," urbicide is accomplished not just through bombardment, bulldozing, and destruction of the built environment; the "killing of cities" is also achieved by inscribing the values and logic of warfare, conflict, and militarism in the very intimate, visceral, and sensed fabric of the city. Take the example of the city of Mostar in Bosnia and Herzegovina, which became the site of severe urbicide during the 1990s. There, in the decades following the official ceasefire, the politics of carving out geopolitical and ethno-national territories has continued in the absence of tanks, checkpoints, and barricades. The war, once perceived as a transient conflict, is in fact intricately woven into the material and emotional landscapes of daily urban life. The subtle nuances of everyday emotions and affect as well as the distinctive ways in which feelings intertwine with the rhythms of city life need to be understood as profound, yet elusive, terrains of geopolitics (Laketa, 2016). The embodied registers of fear, insecurity, and vague but visceral sensations of bodily discomfort shape the ambient contours of urban space well after the dramatic violence stops. These shifting, indeterminate, and embodied ambient conditions are vital in carving out ethno-national identities and territories and reproducing ethno-national fault lines in the city. In Mostar, as well as in other post-conflict cities in the Balkans region, the conflict continues to reverberate throughout everyday spaces and emotional landscapes of malls, schools, boulevards, and bridges (Laketa, 2016, 2018; Carabelli, 2018; Gusic, 2019; Miller and Laketa, 2019; Kadich, 2021). In these cities, and in numerous other war-torn cities and places across global urban peripheries, geopolitical violence is sustained and contested in the spaces of people's lives, from the intimate space of the body (Shalhoub-Kevorkian, 2017; Hammami, 2019) to that of homes and domestic spaces (Jansen, 2015; Belcher, 2018; Azzouz, 2023). In theorizing with war-torn cities, we can also understand how urbicide can be a form of slow violence, achieved through environmental and infrastructural decay and abandonment. As Katherine McKittrick (2011) argues, this slow infrastructural abandonment is an urbicidal practice given that it destroys a sense of place, as is particularly evident among Black communities in the Americas (see also Alves, 2021). Urbicidal geographies—environments altered to destroy or undermine the social and physical fabric of urban heterogeneity—are thus much more insidious, less visible, and, therefore, difficult to grasp.

Affective atmospheres: feminist engagements

Drawing from these knowledges from and with war-torn cities, the book foregrounds "affective atmospheres" as relations of force in and through which urbicidal geographies are unfolding. The term refers to unstructured and fleeting spatial phenomena, such as moods, ambiances, or auras. They signify experiential dimensions of space and place that are often difficult to pin down and describe (Anderson, 2009; Stewart, 2011; Adey et al, 2013; Gandy, 2017). Importantly, an affective atmosphere is not a thing or an object that a place can have (Ahmed, 2004a); rather, atmospheres denote relations that emerge in contact between different bodies—human bodies but also non-human bodies and objects (Anderson, 2009). Inspired by feminist approaches, the book specifies affective atmospheres as ways of inhabiting space and place that are not reducible to conscious actions and perceptions, but instead are fleeting, unspecified, and somewhat indeterminate intensities that impinge upon the body.

Focusing on affective atmospheres allows us to connect seemingly disparate places and cities, tracing relational geographies between urban peripheries and metropolitan centers. It also allows us to explore warfare as an enduring condition in ways that reference theories and knowledges developed with war-torn cities. Specifically, atmospheres are not fixed entities or bounded objects of scholarly analysis, but rather their ontological status is shifting and unfixed. Atmospheres refer to processual and performative relations that are co-constituted in contact between different bodies—both human and non-human ones. They are relational constellations that shape the boundaries of the field of social possibilities (Böhme, 2017). Such an approach to atmospheres builds on Spinoza's understanding of affect as "modifications of the body by which the power of action on the body is increased or diminished" (Spinoza, 1959, cited in Ahmed, 2004b: 4). In other words, affect does not refer to bounded and individual feelings that are "contained" within our human bodies and subjectivities, but rather to collective and shared phenomena. Affect as a bodily capacity to act is also a spatially constituted relation given that it informs embodied orientations in space and habitual performative spatial practices (Ahmed, 2006). The notion of affective atmospheres highlights the spatial dimension of bodily capacities; it attends to the affective tonality of a place. Atmospheres are crucial in understanding how we engage in "relationship to the surfaces, bodies and objects that make up our dwelling places" (Ahmed, 2004b: 27). Affective atmospheres are therefore spatial phenomena—they shape the contours of social space and are in turn shaped by the space.

Affective atmospheres are conceptualized as shared, material, and social constellations, rather than private moods. As such, affective atmospheres are both productive of social and political relations and produced by them, which makes them crucial for understanding the contemporary power dynamics. Here, attention is called to the question of power that conditions, shapes, and assembles affective atmospheres as spatially situated intensities of feeling. For many scholars, the ephemeral qualities of affect and atmospheres are key in understanding the processes and manifestations of sociocultural power beyond the discursive domain (Ahmed, 2004b; Berlant, 2011; Colls, 2012; Anderson, 2017). Or, put succinctly, the experience itself is considered an expression of power.

In attending to the power-laden nature of atmosphere, the book addresses the intersection of affective atmospheres with geopolitical violence, drawing on feminist engagements with the geopolitical. Feminist scholarship has in recent decades extensively examined the significance of bodies, emotions/affect, domestic spaces, and daily life in shaping power dynamics, inequalities, and the construction of war, territory, borders, statehood, and national identity (Dowler and Sharp, 2001; Cowen and Gilbert, 2008; Shalhoub-Kevorkian, 2009; Dixon and Marston, 2011; Pain, 2015; Gökarıksel and Secor, 2020). Emphasizing material relations on the ground, feminist geopolitics rejects predetermined power relations, acknowledging bodies, both human and non-human, as active agents shaping our geopolitical worlds. In doing so, this scholarship sets the groundwork for conceptualizing the complex intersection between atmospheres as ontologically indeterminate relations and geopolitical power. Specifically, this approach rejects the notion of a preestablished system of power, seeking to transcend the binary of hegemony and resistance. It underscores that (geopolitical) power is not simply imposed upon intimate lives, but actively shaped by the intimate sphere itself (Berlant, 1998; Barabantseva et al, 2021). As atmospheres are materialized through routinized arrangements of bodies, objects, and spaces, they are shaped and congealed through habitual actions. There is no power, either hegemonic power or resistance, that finds itself external to atmospheres. Different bodies, objects, and discourses are always already immersed in the performative materialization of atmospheres, where relations of force arise immanently. Questions of power are integral in the production and reproduction of atmospheric relations, with power referring back to the Spinozian question of what a body can do and what relations it can forge.

To grasp ontologically unstable relations such as affective atmospheres, the book considers three interrelated layers as elements that co-constitute atmospheric relations. First, it considers political, legal, and media discourses on urban public emergencies and different forms of political violence in cities. Second, it explores material urban landscape, including buildings, signs, objects, and bodies that shape the atmospheres of banal warfare. Third, it delves into embodied sensations, perceptions, sentiments, and spatial orientations of residents, and other actors, in urban public space. This epistemological framework allows us to grasp the elusive quality of atmospheres by paying attention to how these different layers are co-constituted, how they work in relation to one another, and how they actively shape and reshape atmospheric relations through reiterative actions. In doing so, we gain a deeper understanding of how the atmosphere itself becomes a crucial factor in the unfolding of urbicidal geographies.

What do cities of banal warfare do?

The book employs a conceptual framework based on the intersection of affective atmospheres and geopolitical violence, developed within post-conflict cities in the Balkans, to understand how militarism is routinely assembled in everyday spaces in the cities of Paris and Brussels. Militarism is here defined as more than simply the encroachment of symbolic and material presence of military logics and values on a range of civilian sites and practices. Indeed, cities and warfare have a symbiotic relationship that is centuries old, defying any straightforward dichotomy between civilian urban life and the military. The book, therefore, approaches militarism as a process through which counterterrorism (as a form of modern warfare) and urban space are co-constituted, to examine their shared logics and to inquire into the workings of these relations of power (Howell, 2018). The exploration of discourses, materialities, and affectivities of militarism in everyday urban life gave rise to the notion of banal warfare. The concept of banality refers to quotidian and repetitive reminders or "flaggings" of warfare in everyday urban spaces. Here, I draw on the work of Cindy Katz (2007), who developed the idea of "banal terrorism" to analyze the everyday manifestations of the threat of terror that contribute to a pervasive sense of fear and insecurity in daily life. Katz builds on Michael Billig's (2010/1995) use of the concept of banality to explain the reproduction of nationalism in day-to-day life as ordinary, often unnoticed and taken-for-granted symbols, words, and images, such as flags and forms of speech, like "*our* team," that constantly recreate national identity and belonging to the nation-state.

Departing from their arguments, the book seeks to underscore the importance of examining the less overt but deeply impactful ways that relations of militarism and warfare shape everyday life in cities. It contends that warfare in the city is performatively constituted through daily, habitual, and embodied practices.[1] In other words, it addresses doings, sayings, and embodied orientations that bring into being the notion of warfare and continue to do so through repeated, often ritualized, and unconscious rearticulations. Such enactments of warfare and militarism are inherently unstable and incomplete performative acts, thus opening the spaces of non-normative atmospherics, or an "atmospheric otherwise" (Simmons, 2017).

To fully grasp what cities of banal warfare *do*—that is, what political work they perform—the book considers the intersection of three layers as analytical elements that work simultaneously and in relation to one another: the discourses on urban warfare, the built environment of the city, and the felt and sensorial experiences that accompany daily urban life. The following chapters seeks to synthesize the complex interactions between political discourses, urban landscape, and affective experiences as they come together to shape and reshape atmospheric relations. In doing so, the chapters aim to discern and provide insight on the multiple forces at play in the formation and dissolution of urban geopolitical tensions and subjectivities. Notably, the book highlights how these entangled mechanisms of power are forging everyday, intimate spaces and subjectivities. It sheds light on how cities shape the notion of warfare, and vice versa, in the intimacy of the everyday.

Notes on the method

The book draws on several different sources, from the analysis of government, media, and policy documents to interviews with key urban governance and civil society actors, including members of the police, town planners, elected city officials, social workers, staff at city tourist offices, and others engaging in various ways with "countering terrorism" in the cities of Paris and Brussels. Furthermore, the project included participant observation and walk-alongs (Kusenbach, 2003) with residents of the two cities, conducted at various points between 2016 and 2023; these attended to the felt geographies of everyday life amid different forms of urban violence.

To situate urban geopolitics in place and within the everyday, participant observations and walk-alongs concentrated on the areas surrounding two squares: the Place de la République in Paris and the Place de la Bourse/Beursplein in Brussels. These areas were chosen for the following reasons. Both stand at specific "neuralgic" points in the urban geography of the two cities, especially after the attacks in 2015. The Place de la République is situated between the 10th and 11th arrondissements (districts), where the massacres at Charlie Hebdo, the Bataclan, and several bars and restaurants took place; these attacks targeted everyday places and residents of the city. Similarly, the Place de la Bourse/Beursplein is situated between the municipality of Ville de Bruxelles/Stad Brussel (the so-called Brussel Mille) and the municipality of Molenbeek-Saint-Jean/Sint-Jans-Molenbeek, which has been labeled the "enemy territory" in the ongoing war on terror. Following the attacks, both squares became a place where people started to spontaneously gather to mourn, organize vigils, and share memories of their loved ones. In Paris, residents wrote messages and placed mementos on the 19th-century bronze statue of Marianne, the personification of the French Republic, in the middle of the square. And in Brussels, an impromptu memorial space was assembled in the area in front of the 19th-century Brussels Stock Exchange building, on the southeastern side of the square, and on the building staircase, which is surrounded by neo-Renaissance statues of baby angels and lions. Moreover, both places have been the site of public protest in the cities, especially important given their symbolic significance in representing national and republican values. This is particularly the case with the Place de la République, which has long been used for public protests in Paris. These considerations are relevant insofar as militarism infuses the notion of public order in the city, as discussed later. The micro focus on these squares and the surrounding areas serves to anchor and localize the discourses surrounding urban warfare within the context of everyday environments, shedding light on how warfare permeates the ordinary, intertwining with the mundane aspects of city life.

The aim of the walk-alongs was to delve into everyday affective and sensorial experiences that accompany life in the city (Rose et al, 2010; Degen and Rose, 2012; Dowling et al, 2017; Duru, 2019). Specifically, the project relies on formulations of discomfort, rather than insecurity, to explore the affective geographies of the squares and the surrounding areas; this was based on my work in (post)war cities in Bosnia and Herzegovina (Laketa, 2016, 2018), where feelings of direct threat and insecurity have given way to more ambiguous and fleeting experiences of discomfort. The focus on discomfort opens up a wider and more subtle terrain of exploration of affective geographies, as it does not rely exclusively on already meaning-laden state discourse on insecurity and vigilance (for further discussion on the politics of discomfort, see Chadwick, 2021; Smith et al, 2021). The participants in the walk-alongs in or around the squares were chosen in various ways—some were selected randomly through direct contact on the square, some were contacted through friend networks, and some were contacted as members of various neighborhood initiatives working toward different cultural, social, economic, and political ends. The interviews with key actors and the walk-alongs with residents were conducted in different languages—some in English, some in French with the help of a research assistant, and some in my native Bosnian, Croatian, and Serbian.

During the walk-alongs, the participants would first choose their favorite or everyday route or location. In Paris, walks took place around the Place de la République, and in Brussels, they were in the Place de la Bourse and the surrounding areas of the Brussel Mille and the municipality of Molenbeek. During the walks, participants would talk about what they liked and didn't like about their chosen location or route. Sometimes the walk-alongs covered several kilometers, but at other times they were relatively stationary. We would delve further into feelings of (dis)comfort, sometimes by experimenting with visually representing how (dis)comfort looks and feels in the city. For example, during the walks, some participants took photos or short video clips of objects, places, or moments that they associated with (dis)comfort and insecurity. Following the walk, we would usually sit down and further discuss feelings of (in)security and personal or shared experiences of violence and threat, more specifically related to the threat of terrorism. Some interviews took place on a single occasion and some developed over two or more occasions, each lasting one to three hours. Through participant observation, interviews, and walk-alongs, I began to explore the assembling of affective atmospheres, keeping in mind their shifting, porous, and indeterminate qualities (Wetherell, 2013; Sumartojo and Pink, 2018).

The book draws on these various sources to understand the following: first, what discourses on warfare in the city circulate among differently positioned urban governance actors; second, how the material landscape of the city (including bodies, objects, and the built environment) performatively (re)creates the notion of ongoing urban warfare; third, how sensorial experiences and embodied subjectivities are enrolled in the state project of countering terrorism; and, fourth, what the everyday and embodied practices and affectivities of undoing and unsettling urban warfare are. Importantly, the different cities and locations are not used in a comparative fashion that views cities and places as discrete units (Robinson, 2016). Rather, the aim is to trace the relational geographies of the urban as they are complexly interwoven across different forms of geopolitical violence and militarism—in other words, how the events, discourses, and sentiments in one location travel to, arise in, and spill over into another location. I track articulations of urban warfare as they reverberate across different urban areas, and in doing so, I aim to position different cities and places in relation to one another.

Overview of the book

Cities of Banal Warfare develops in the following manner. Chapter 2 traces the legal, political, and dominant media discourses that have shaped the narrative of urban warfare in the cities of Paris and Brussels throughout the 21st century. It focuses on the legal frameworks of the state of emergency and the lockdown, implemented in response to various events identified as a threat to public order in the cities. The discourses on warfare play a pivotal role in influencing public perception, policy decisions, and the very nature of urban planning. The chapter thus addresses in depth the first layer or element that is crucial in the process of shaping and reshaping affective atmospheres—the discursive layer.

Chapter 3 addresses the second layer—the built environment. This chapter examines the material landscape through which the city of banal warfare is brought into being. The aim is to localize and ground discourses on urban warfare in the everyday environment, beyond the notion of the emergency, exception, and crisis. Besides the more visible enactments of urban warfare—such as the deployment of heavily armed police and military on streets and squares and the presence of military-grade equipment—attention is turned to seemingly more innocuous "flaggings" or reminders of urban threat, from bollards, trash cans and plants to various advertisements. Moreover, the chapter addresses the recent urban redevelopment initiatives that reinstate the notion of the city at war through capital-intensive private market interventions and neoliberal processes of gentrification.

Chapter 4 explores the third layer shaping affective atmospheres—the sensorial and affective experiences that underpin everyday life in the cities of banal warfare. The chapter addresses two government initiatives that during the research period formed part of the psychological dimensions of urban warfare. One is an effort to mobilize the affective state of vigilance and the second is an effort to counter so-called radicalization. The chapter argues that these recently revamped urban security governance agendas further intervene on the level of the body, the sensate, and the atmospheric. The chapter ends by synthesizing how the three interrelated layers come together to shape atmospheric relations, arguing that the affective atmospheres are enrolled by the state to serve at the front line of the battle against "the enemy within."

Chapter 5 considers everyday practices of undermining and undoing geopolitical violence and building a notion of everyday peace in the city. While Chapters 2 to 4 foreground how the logic of warfare and militarism becomes inscribed in the material, social, and sensorial fabric of the city, Chapter 5 outlines forms of atmospheric labor as performative assembly of atmospheres of mutual interconnectedness and vulnerability. The chapter addresses notions of embodied peace that are mobilized in cities to reshape war atmospherics, arguing that the spaces and practices involved in mitigating geopolitical violence are frequently overlooked and concealed.

The conclusion highlights key features of the banality of urban warfare that has become a protracted and durable condition through affective geographies and ways of feelings that accompany everyday life in the city. It further considers these developments as forms of urbicidal geographies and argues that the military logics underscoring notions of permanent threat support an "us" versus "them" mentality, justifies the use of force and violence, and ultimately deepens social inequalities.

TWO

Urban Warfare: From State of Emergency to Lockdown

A key feature of cities of banal warfare is the process of framing different forms of political violence and urban public emergencies as acts of war. The language used to depict various violent events and threats shapes the way these events are interpreted; it guides thoughts, actions, emotions, and responses. The notion of warfare is increasingly deployed as a framing device for interpreting urban public emergencies. This language dominates political speeches, saturates the media landscape, and directs legal discourses. The chapter thus begins by analyzing the way wars are waged in cities through dominant legal, political, and media discourses in the city. These discourses result in different events being "recognized" as acts of warfare, further legitimizing specific political actions, legal policies, and urban governance initiatives. The language of militarism shapes the way cities are imagined and governed. Through this language, the city becomes framed as a battleground in the fight between an often invisible "enemy." Cities are imagined as unruly spaces of violence, disease, and decay that threaten the stability of the political and public order. If cities are under siege, then political responses are framed by the need to bunker and fortress. Therefore, more than simply a language of war, discourses on militarism shape urban governance agendas and re-configure everyday urban spaces. The following sections turn to analyzing several different events in Paris and Brussels as instances that helped propel the notion of urban warfare and which further work to normalize it in urban spaces.

State of emergency: from sustaining colonial powers to governing the urban metropolis

The language of warfare, in the case of Paris, is deeply intertwined with the invocation and the implementation of the French legal framework of state of emergency. A state of emergency was declared in Paris and mainland France in response to the following events: the revolt in the suburbs of Paris, and other French cities, in November 2005; the attacks on sports halls, music venues, restaurants, and bars in Paris on November 13, 2015; and the COVID-19 pandemic in March 2020. These interrelated events of the enforcement of a state of emergency, I argue, are key moments of discursive alignment between militarism and urban governance in the city. Therefore, it is worth taking a close look at this legal measure that the state has continued to revert to in recent decades.

The legislation put into effect during the three occasions is based on the State of Emergency Act (Loi relative à l'état d'urgence) – a law adopted by the French Parliament in 1955 as a response to the Algerian War of Independence. The "state of emergency" (*l'état d'urgence*) can be declared by the president of the republic at the Council of Ministers when there is an "imminent danger resulting from serious breaches of public order or events which, because of their nature or severity, constitute public calamities" (State of Emergency Act 1955; own translation). Among other things, the State of Emergency Act accords "exceptional powers" (*pouvoirs exceptionnels*) to the president of the republic. It further gives authority to the minister of interior and to prefects to conduct house searches and house arrests without judiciary oversight, ban public gatherings, regulate or ban the circulation of people and/or vehicles, and enforce curfews. It also permits military authorities to take police powers, if necessary. The

1955 law is an adaptation of the earlier legislation on *l'état de siège* (state of siege), that deals specifically with war and armed insurrection. At the time of the Algerian War, the French colonial state wanted to avoid calling this an act of war, instead choosing euphemistic terms such as "*événements d'Algérie*" (events in Algeria) and "*rébellion en Algérie*" (rebellion in Algeria; Rousseau, 2006); therefore, they developed a new law on the state of emergency which did not differ much from the martial law formulated as the state of siege. Even Edgar Faure, the prime minister of France at the time, who was responsible for putting the law in front of Parliament, later admitted "the simple truth that the term 'state of siege' irresistibly evokes war and ... any allusion to war had to be carefully avoided in connection with the Algerian affairs" (Faure, 1982: 197; own translation; see also Rousseau, 2006). The state of emergency was thus a way for the French colonial state to secure and sustain its war powers and violently suppress the former colony's claim for independence (Blanchard, 2018).

Two decades after the war in Algeria, a state of emergency was activated during secessionist movements in New Caledonia in 1984. However, at the beginning of the 21st century, the state of emergency legislation gradually came to be a way to govern urban affairs in mainland France, in addition to being used to deal with its "overseas" colonies (the latest declaration of the state of emergency in New Caledonia, as of the time of writing, was in May 2024). The first time this law was implemented in mainland France was during the urban unrest in the fall of 2005 (Thénault, 2007). The revolts were a response to the deaths of Zyed Benna and Bouna Traoré in the Paris suburb of Clichy-sous-Bois. The two teenage boys died tragically while attempting to escape from the police, who were notorious for their violent stop and search practices (Fassin, 2011). The boys' deaths sparked mass public protests in Paris and later in other French cities, a revolt that at times turned to violence and included the burning of cars and buildings, leading to over 2,500 arrests. About ten days after the start of the revolt, President Jacques Chirac declared a state of emergency that lasted several weeks. This event set the stage for the use of the colonial wartime law on the state of emergency to control cities and govern urban spaces in mainland France. The urban unrest was thus interpreted as an insurgency, requiring the implementation of a colonial military intervention. More than that, the state of emergency as a counterinsurgency enabled the authorities to control the residents of suburban areas of Paris who have long been subjected to discourses and practices of racialization and othering (Khiari, 2009). It was, in a sense, a declaration of war on racialized and impoverished communities that Nicolas Sarkozy, the minister of the interior at the time, called "*racaille*"—a racialized term broadly meaning thug. With Sarkozy's further calls to "*nettoyer au Kärcher*" (thoroughly clean) the suburbs, we see also the racialized imaginative geographies of the urban space itself. Drawing on the work of Said (1979), imaginative geographies are sociocultural representations of places as binary depictions that articulate the grids of imperialist power between colonized peripheries and the imperial center. The imaginative geographies, especially of urban areas, constructing the notion of "homeland" cities and "terrorist" cities, have long informed the global war on terror. As Graham notes, such urban imaginative geographies "do geopolitical work by designating the familiar space inhabited by a putative 'us', and opposing it to the unfamiliar geographies inhabited by a putative Other — the 'them' who become the legitimate target for military or colonial power" (2006: 255). In the case of Paris, the colonial war-time logic of governing urban unrest thus further facilitated the imperialist imaginative geographies through depictions of the working-class neighborhoods in the city (the so-called *quartier populaires*) as orientalized spaces of violence and decay (Dikeç, 2011).

Cities in lockdown

Ten years after the urban unrest in 2005, a state of emergency was declared for the second time in metropolitan France. This was triggered by events on the evening of November 13, 2015, when several armed groups and suicide bombers enacted a coordinated attack on the Stade de France, the Bataclan concert hall, and several restaurants and bars located in the 10th and 11th arrondissements. The mass indiscriminate shooting of concertgoers and people sitting in bars, restaurants, and other public places left 130 people, together with several of the attackers, killed. At midnight, President François Hollande announced a state of emergency, which this time lasted for two years. The state also quickly deployed combat troops to patrol the streets of Paris and other cities in France as part of Opération Sentinelle (Operation Sentinel). The military operation had been launched in January that year following mass murders at the Charlie Hebdo magazine headquarters and a kosher supermarket. However, after the November events, the military presence rose to 10,000 troops deployed nationwide, with about 6,500 of them in the Paris area. It was the largest military operation on mainland France since World War II, with more than half of the active French troops assigned to domestic patrols (Ministère des Armées, nd).

One day after the attacks on November 13 in Paris, as the streets remained mostly empty aside from people laying flowers for the victims, several house raids took place 300 kilometers away in Molenbeek, a municipality in Brussels, with police apprehending five people as suspects in the Paris shootings. In the week after the Paris attacks and the raids in Molenbeek, Belgian security forces intercepted a vague SMS that, in the words of the local newspaper, "plunged Brussels into fear" (Lasoen, 2017: 13). Though ambiguous, the SMS was suspicious enough to raise the security level across the Brussels-Capital Region to level 4, the maximum level. Belgium's Coordination Unit for Threat Assessment set the alarm at level 4 due to the possibility of an attack similar to what had taken place in Paris. Koen Geens, the minister of justice at the time, advised the population to stay vigilant in light of a "serious and imminent threat" against the city

(Ponsaers and Devroe, 2017). The government also decided to take the drastic measure of completely shutting down the city to prevent an event like the one in Paris. Without much explanation, Brussels was placed in lockdown, an intervention that was, at the time, unprecedented at the level of an entire city. It started off with the closure of public schools, followed by the shutting down of the transportation system, the closure of other public buildings and services, including universities, and finally the closure of cafes, shops, and restaurants in the city. Citizens were advised to stay home until the lockdown was lifted, which as it turned out was five days later, when the security threat was lowered to level 3, again without much explanation from the government.

Just a few months later, with many residents of Brussels still recovering from these traumatic events, another violent and coordinated assault occurred in the city. On the morning of March 22, 2016, a large detonation struck Brussels' Zaventem airport. Two nail bombs carried by three suicide bombers, all residents of Brussels, exploded in the departure hall. An hour later, a deadly attack occurred at the Maalbeek metro station, with two assailants killing 35 people and injuring many more. The security alert across Belgium was raised to the maximum, and again Brussels was placed in lockdown. Residents were advised to stay indoors and communicate via social networks or SMS. Public transportation was shut down, flights were cancelled, and public buildings were closed. The sudden surge in communication as people tried to check on loved ones and secure their own safety overwhelmed cell phone networks, leading to widespread service crashes. The streets of the city became jammed with cars as residents sought to flee or find safer spaces. On March 25, the threat level was lowered to level 3, indicating a possible and probable threat, an assessment that stayed in place for the next two years.

Paris and Brussels thus became entangled in the geography of non-state violence perpetrated by indiscriminate killings in urban public spaces, with the assaults organized or inspired by the Islamic State militant group, which was fighting predominantly in Syria at the time. Moreover, the urban and state responses to these assaults unfolded along the Paris–Brussels axis. Besides the coordination of police and security intelligence between the two cities, additional widespread urban and state government interventions in the two cities were often mirrored. Therefore, similar to France's Opération Sentinelle, Belgium launched its own homeland military operation, named Operation Vigilant Guardian. Soldiers patrolled the streets of Brussels and protected so-called high-value targets, such as EU buildings, embassies, and other institutions. By October 2016, three quarters of Belgian armed forces (around 1,800 soldiers) were tasked with this homeland military operation, rather than being deployed on their external missions (La Défense, nd). While the number of soldiers fluctuated, the operation continued uninterrupted for five years, until September 2021.

In both cities, the attacks were met with heavy-handed military and police interventions that had wide-reaching effects on the reorganization of the cities, and the consequent urban imaginaries. These measures aimed primarily to "harden" and fortify urban spaces. The measures of lockdown and state of emergency have historically been employed as state-sanctioned responses to wartime conditions and armed conflicts. Lockdowns, in particular, have served as security measures against various threats, including terrorism, warfare, prison unrest, and infectious diseases (Sudbury, 2005; Morin, 2013). Lockdown operates as a spatial intervention geared towards curtailing movement and minimizing social interaction. By imposing restrictions on mobility and social gatherings, lockdowns, and states of emergency, seek to assert authority over space, shaping the urban environment into a controlled and regulated domain where movement and interaction are curtailed in the pursuit of maintaining security and public safety. The vision of a total control of mobility informs the construction of urban imaginary geographies of a "segmented, immobile, frozen space" (Foucault, 1977: 195). Thus, both measures rely on the spatial logics of enclosure, fortification, and immobility to secure the city in a situation of immanent urban warfare.

Waging wars in cities

In both cities, the violent killings were framed as an act of war, requiring military intervention. Moreover, shortly after the attacks in Paris, in his address to the French Parliament on November 15, 2015, President François Hollande was clear: "*La France est en guerre. Les actes commis vendredi soir à Paris et près du Stade de France, sont des actes de guerre*" (France is at war. The acts committed in Paris and near the Stade de France on Friday evening are acts of war). Indeed, a month earlier, the president had already announced the "*une guerre total*" (total war) while speaking in the European Parliament. Since the attackers who committed the massacres were mostly French and Belgian citizens, who were either inspired by or organized through the Islamic State militant group fighting in Syria, this gave rise to the notion of the "enemy within." Manuel Valls, French interior minister, referred to this "*ennemi intérieur*" (internal enemy) as "barbarians in hiding" and a new threat facing what he called "European values" (Le Monde, 2013). The figure of the "enemy within" (Rigouste, 2009) is here rooted in the cultural dimensions of the war on terror as a war over values and culture that relies on the "clash of civilizations" discourse between "us" and "them," "our" and "their" values (Bhattacharyya, 2013; Kundnani, 2014; Li, 2019). This discourse further constructs the figure of the enemy through the processes of gendering and racialization that frame an orientalist notion of the terrorist, as part of ongoing nation-building processes (Puar, 2018/2007).

The municipality of Molenbeek, the suburban areas of Paris, and other racialized and impoverished urban areas throughout France and Belgium became the "enemy" territory as the wartime rhetoric further fueled nationalistic discourses based on "us" versus "them." The result was military-style raids launched on several of these urban areas in the days following the November 13 attacks, including the infamous raid at the Parisian suburb of St Denis, when the police and the military fired some 5,000 rounds of ammunition at a building where three suspects were identified. Most raids, however, were conducted without finding any suspects or criminal activities. Besides raids, the police in the two cities conducted house searches, detentions, and stop and search as part of their counterterrorism response. These measures predominantly targeted Muslim residents and other racialized communities in the cities (Human Rights Watch, 2016a, 2016b). The state of emergency legislation in Paris further allowed searches without warrants, which resulted in more than 4,000 house searches during the two years of the emergency, with over 700 house arrests ordered (Hergon, 2021). As the police were breaking down doors and conducting searches, they targeted people often without having sufficient evidence to reasonably classify them as potential security threats. The indiscriminate, violent, and excessive policing of the Muslim and other racialized communities is evident in the modest and limited number of actual convictions on the grounds of terrorism (Human Rights Watch, 2016a; Mechaï and Hergon, 2020).

In addition to turning streets into battlefields in mainland France, in the days following the attacks on November 13, the government launched air strikes targeting the city of Raqqa, dropping about 20 bombs on the suspected headquarters of the Islamic State militant group in Syria. Both France and Belgium formed part of a US-led coalition, code-named Operation Inherent Resolve, launched in September 2014 against the Islamic State. The air strikes continued in the years that followed, culminating in the bombing of Raqqa in the summer and fall of 2017. The fighting destroyed 80 percent of the city (United Nations Institute for Training and Research, 2017); an Amnesty International investigation reported 1,600 civilian deaths in the city resulting from the strikes by the coalition forces (Amnesty International, 2018a).

The urbicide of Raqqa resonates with the further militarization of the notion of public order on the homeland urban warfare front. In Paris, to begin with, the State of Emergency Act provides the groundwork for establishing the disturbance of public order as a declaration of war. It identifies as the enemy all people whose "behavior constitute a threat to security and public order" (State of Emergency Act, 1955; own translation) and are thus subjected to extrajudicial house searches and house arrest. Furthermore, the militarist notion of public order prompted further use of military-style equipment by police forces in the cities. This has led to a steady increase over the years in the use of military chemical and explosive weapons to secure urban public order, especially during public demonstrations. According to ACAT France (2020), the use of tear gas and other forms of supposedly nonlethal ammunition has continually increased: in 2018 alone they registered a 296 percent increase in the use of sting ball grenades (a weapon used to disperse crowds, these emit a loud detonation sound, beyond the threshold of pain, and at the same time disperse more than a dozen rubber pellets, which scatter in all direction. The use of the weapon can sometimes cause serious and even irreversible damage such as severed ligaments and nerves, hearing damage, as well as permanent mutilation of the face, in particular the eyes, leading to total or partial loss of use of an eye). As an example, in just one day, December 1, 2018, the police fired 339 GLI-F4 grenades during a "yellow vest" public demonstration in Paris. The infamous GLI-F4 grenades contain 25 grams of the powerful explosive TNT, acting both as a tear gas and a grenade, an explosive ammunition which, since 2020, has been banned from use in France due to long-standing outcry from human rights groups, journalists, and lawyers.

The two years of the state of emergency ended with the passing of a new law that entrenched the conditions of the state of emergency. The new anti-terrorism law that came into effect in November 2017 incorporated several measures originally authorized only as an emergency arrangement, such as searching homes and ordering house arrests without full prior procedural safeguards (Amnesty International, 2018b). The justification for the new law was that, in the words of the interior minister, Gérard Collomb: "We're still in a state of war" (Jarry, 2017). This shift marked the normalization of the emergency measures and the notion of urban warfare that continues to this day. The Loi relative à la sécurité globale (Law on Global Security), passed in 2021, is just the latest iteration of the wartime logic, giving more autonomy to the police and permitting the use of drones for surveillance of urban public space, among other things.

Militarism and COVID-19 lockdowns

The third state of emergency was announced at the start of the COVID-19 pandemic, in March 2020. With President Emmanuel Macron's repeated proclamations that "*nous sommes en guerre*" (we are at war), the language of warfare and militarism soon became a prominent discourse during the public health crisis.[1] As such, it triggered another installation of military logics governing both public order and public health (Laketa and Fregonese, 2023). The "insurgent" virus became anthropomorphized as an actor threatening the stability of "our" social, political, and economic order. The much-circulated picture of the virus with threatening red spikes served to put a visible "face" on an otherwise invisible "enemy" that was "infiltrating" bodies, cities, and countries and which the state was calling to "eliminate."

Even though the law was changed slightly to account for public health—it was now called a *l'état d'urgence sanitaire* (health state of emergency)—the underlying military logics of control of public space, regulation or banning of circulation, and stay-at-home orders remained the same. This type of state power to contain and remove became globally known as the "lockdown." While the scope and duration of the counterterror lockdowns in Brussels in 2015 and 2016 had at the time constituted an unprecedented state security intervention in a post-1945 European city, since then, various forms of urban lockdown, albeit with more limited scope and duration, have been employed in responding to security threats, such as the lockdown in London in 2017 following the Westminster Bridge attack. Indeed, the UK's National Counter Terrorism Security Office has recently added lockdown as one of the "highly effective" counterterrorism measures (National Counter Terrorism Security Office, 2022). Lockdown as a political strategy for governing emergencies has become an increasingly acceptable security measure by states to govern a variety of threats and emergencies, culminating with the implementation of COVID-19 lockdowns imposed globally across many countries and cities.

Bringing into conversation the notions of lockdown and state of emergency imposed as responses to the COVID-19 pandemic in France and Belgium shows further productive connections between the governmentality of disease and the governmentality of terrorism. The vision of total control of mobility in the city is also one of main spatial logics driving the implementation of COVID-19 lockdowns. The suspension of movement ensures command of urban public spaces identified as vulnerable spaces of contagion. Moreover, with COVID-19 lockdowns in Europe, the suspension of movement has been larger in scope, extending to state borders. Here, the lockdowns entailed a (re)introduction of an array of border materialities—fences, barbed wire, and other militarist, often haphazardly implemented, barriers in border regions—that had become obsolete, at least within the EU (Fall, 2020). The state enclosures entailed the blockade of long-eliminated borders within the different states of the EU and an even greater solidification on the outer rim of "fortress Europe." The reinstatement of state borders further catalyzed state nationalist discourses on the defense of the health of the nation in the "war against the virus" (Diaz and Mountz, 2020), and the implementation of lockdowns relied on racialized and colonial ideas of contagious "others" (Mitropoulos, 2020).

The spatial logic of the lockdown, which centers on processes of fortification and enclosure, corresponds to a wider military gaze governing urban space. It enables the framing of public health as a matter of national security in everyday (urban) environments. Therefore, more than a language of war, state responses to the COVID-19 virus included a host of military and state security infrastructures, technologies, and personnel deployed as emergency measures. In France and Belgium, again, military personnel were tasked with supporting local death management and vaccine rollout, transporting patients, and patrolling the streets to ensure compliance with the lockdown regulations. Thus, the militarist response to the pandemic was more than discursive; it also entailed the material and the social presence of a warlike situation. In other words, the framing of the pandemic as a national security threat mobilized the practices and values of militarism as a response to the constructed threat.

This militarism of the state response to a health crisis has impacted different communities in different ways. During COVID-19 lockdowns, under the conditions of expansion of what is considered criminal behavior, such as not observing social hygiene rules and mobility restrictions, we witnessed increased policing of the already vulnerable and stigmatized urban populations in both Paris and Brussels (De Backer and Melgaço, 2021). Many human rights organizations identified several abuses of police powers in poorer racialized neighborhoods (Amnesty International, 2020; Police Watch, 2020), as the notion of the health crisis as an act of war further reactivated racial and colonial imaginaries of danger, disease, and threat (Mitropoulos, 2020). The coupling of health and security further sustains and naturalizes these forms of militarism (Loyd, 2009). Lockdown as a governance framework can therefore be seen along a continuum of colonial and racial forms of governing, and as such it compounds existing inequalities.

The emergent entanglement of terror and the virus promotes an understanding of security and risk in ways that are partial, labelling some communities as sources of risk in ways that promote mistrust and supports forms of populist nationalism. The "us versus them" mentality of warfare shapes the solutions to crisis in ways that prevent cooperation. Finally, with the links between the governing of microbial and terrorist threats, militarism becomes sutured into everyday life, shaping embodied understandings and performances of security, risk, vulnerability, and threat.

From the exceptional to the everyday

This chapter has looked at the dominant discourses on warfare that are implemented to interpret and frame different public emergencies and events (Butler, 2016/2009). From the legal framework of the state of emergency to the discourses and practices of lockdown, it has demonstrated the implementation of the military logic of urban governance, wherein a broad range of public emergencies and urban conflicts are treated as an act of war. This has led to the normalization of militarist practices and values across an extended range of spaces and social relations. Waging wars deepens social stratification and disintegration, a lesson learned from numerous cities afflicted by war (Maček, 2009; Enloe, 2010; Fregonese, 2019; Kaldor and Sassen, 2020). Wars fuel racism, xenophobic nationalism, and autocracy. Using the notion of warfare as a framing device in the cities of Paris and Brussels has reinforced division among fractured communities; it has promoted mistrust and exacerbated social discrimination.

To conclude, the continued use of state of emergency and lockdown measures to govern urban conflict and different forms of urban crisis has rendered different military logics and values as a form of common sense when it comes to governing the urban. To be sure, this is not an exclusively French or Belgian predicament, though there is a tendency in popular media discourses to portray French politics and methods of policing as particularly excessive within western Europe. Rather, similar trajectories have been observed and analyzed in other European contexts, including Germany (Krasmann and Hentschel, 2019; von der Burg and Krasmann, 2023), the Netherlands (Fadil et al, 2019), and the UK (Coaffee, 2004, 2021), and there has been a general rise of the national security state throughout Europe (Amnesty International, 2017). The next chapter delves further into the normalization of urban warfare beyond spectacular violent events and into everyday spaces, bodies, and sensations that form the affective atmospheres of the city. These everyday geographies are key in both the reproduction of military logics of the urban and the undoing of the notion of the city at war. In theorizing with war-torn cities, urban conflict is performed and destabilized through daily practices and affective experiences that accompany life in the city. Moreover, it is exactly these affective geographies that are increasingly the target of the military doctrine.

THREE

Everyday Urban Landscapes as Battlescapes

In June 2016, I was walking through a metro station in Brussels when I spotted two heavily armed soldiers standing on the platform. Commuters were passing by the men slowly and quietly (Figure 3.1). After about a week, I had seen numerous military personnel, watched an array of armed vehicles, and observed an assortment of military equipment in the city's public spaces. The residents of Brussels seemed to be getting used to the military presence, with only the occasional tourist taking a snapshot of "the warzone." Three months had passed since the suicide bomb attacks on the Zaventem airport and the Maalbeek metro station, events that caused the loss of numerous lives, left many people injured, and inflicted profound emotional distress on the city's residents. I was in Brussels with my colleague Sara Fregonese, and we were trying to understand the felt experience of the different counterterrorist security measures rapidly being put in place (for further information on our joint preliminary study, see Fregonese and Laketa, 2022). We asked ourselves: What does the presence of military bodies and objects *do* in urban public places?

A Brussels federal police officer involved in the antiterrorist unit told us during an interview: "Are we going to prevent a bomb attack because there's military in the metro? No!" He then proceeded to explain: "It's a political decision, to reassure the public, to let them know we are doing all

Figure 3.1: Brussels metro, June 2016

Source: Author's own

we can." The military bodies and objects thus served as a visual reminder of the state's presence in those spaces, rather than attending to a particular security task. More than that, their visual presence enacted a specific understanding of the meaning of those bomb attacks as an act of war, as well as of the meaning of security in the city. If "we are at war," how are the residents being reassured of their safety amid the ongoing urban warfare?

In addressing these questions, this chapter focuses on the implementation of counterterror measures in everyday public places, beyond mediatized geopolitical violence and emergencies. It traces how discourses about permanent warfare, discussed in the previous chapter, became materialized in urban spaces in the months and years following the violent emergencies and crisis events in Paris and Brussels. Using the concept of performativity, the chapter examines the mundane ways the notion of warfare is constantly and routinely reproduced in the city in the aftermath of attacks and public emergencies. Specifically, it draws attention to different elements of the material urban landscape—bodies, buildings, and objects—as repetitive and performative enactments of the ongoing urban warfare.

From reassuring the public to cleaning up the city

As noted in the previous chapter, one of the most immediate state responses during the states of emergency and the lockdown was to set up the homeland fronts of urban military operations, code-named Sentinelle and Vigilant Guardian. Armored vehicles were rapidly rolled onto the squares and streets of both Paris and Brussels, and troops were brought back from their "external missions" to patrol the "mainland" metropolises. The engagement of the military, however, extended well beyond emergency measures, and their presence soon became a staple of the everyday urban landscape. It is precisely the soldiers' visibility within the cityscape that provides insights into the role of the military on urban streets, beyond emergency acts. Katz (2007) specifically comments on the soldiers' attire: a camouflaged uniform, theoretically developed for troops to be able to blend in to the battlefield environment. Katz writes in the context of the New York City following the attacks on September 11, 2001:

> Here we have soldiers who have little familiarity with their surroundings cropping up in jungle and desert motifs. ... Their camouflage makes them visible – their bodies emblematic of a muscular state. None of this alters a thing regarding the protection of people and the spaces they traverse. This staging of security does nothing so much as authorize a security state and routinize the ever presence of terrorism in our midst. This routinization engages the popular imaginary and reproduces docility vis à vis the state and its security operations. And this is, of course, the intent of making visible that which is designed for invisibility. (2007: 353)

The camouflaged soldier on city streets is, for Katz, a body that does not blend into the surroundings; rather, the military figure stands out and signals the "always already presence of terrorism" and the warfare "in our midst" (2007: 350). Their routinized daily presence in the city is a constant reminder that the "enemy" is always among "us," however dormant, perhaps in a "sleeper cell." The military's role is thus performative, as their visibility in urban landscape continuously recreates the existence of warfare in the city. In other words, their presence creates the very reality they contest; their occupation of everyday urban spaces constructs the warfare that they ostensibly merely confront. The soldier performatively consolidates warfare in the city through their reiterative presence in daily places.

Returning to the question about how residents are being reassured by the presence of the military, an important point to consider is the symbolic and performative meaning of the soldier as a representative of the state. Military bodies in urban places embody two complementary meanings. One symbolic aspect of the presence of soldiers in the city relates to "reassuring the public" and presenting the image of the protective state. Such is the symbolic role of the military stationed in front of state institutions and inside metro stations, both classified as "high-end targets," identified by the state as places in the city that are vulnerable to "enemy attacks" and thus in need of state protection. The second symbolic aspect of soldiers in the city relates to projecting the image of the strong state, always ready to attack "the enemy within," thus instilling fear in the urban public. As discussed in Chapter 2, discourses on warfare have generated the figures of the "enemy combatant" and the "terrorist," a racialized figure that threatens from inside the state. Armed troops are then deployed to engage in active combat to target those residents who are identified as combatants. This second symbolic aspect underlies the foundation of Plan Canal, one of the Belgian federal government's main counterterrorism measures in the city of Brussels. Initially called Plan Molenbeek, it was among the 18 measures the Belgian government announced on November 19, 2015, immediately after the Paris attacks. The plan primarily aimed to increase police and military presence in the municipality of Molenbeek and later other racialized working-class neighborhoods around the Canal areas of Brussels, areas identified as harboring the "enemy." The increased police and military presence was tasked with patrolling the streets, performing stop and search, and conducting raids and house searches.

Plan Molenbeek, later Plan Canal, was initiated because of the intense political and media attention towards these neighborhoods, which had long been labeled as the "Muslim" areas in the city (Torrekens, 2009). Molenbeek is among 19 municipalities that form the Brussels-Capital Region; it has approximately 100,000 inhabitants and covers an area of about six square kilometers. It is a centrally situated municipality, just west of the city center with the canal, a 19th-century waterway, between the two municipalities. Molenbeek, a former industrial hub, is now characterized by low income levels and high unemployment rates compared to other Brussels neighborhoods (IBSA, nd). As a working-class neighborhood, it attracted migrant workers arriving in the city throughout the 20th century, and it currently houses a large Moroccan community as well as other North African and Eastern European communities (Meeus et al, 2019). In addition to being stigmatized as a poor and migrant neighborhood, in the months and years that followed the 2015 and 2016 attacks, the neighborhood became a convenient placeholder for social problems connected to the spate of indiscriminate murders in public places, constructed as a place of violence and deviance. Molenbeek thus served to spatially contain and territorialize the amorphous threat in the ongoing warfare that the state embarked on. For numerous political leaders and the media, Molenbeek came to spatially represent the failure of "Western" ideals of democracy and multiculturalism; it was viewed as an area harboring values and practices incompatible with the "West" (Voeten, 2015) This "clash of civilizations" discourse was accompanied by a series of metaphors that dehumanized its residents by painting them as religious zealots (France24, 2015) and the area as a "breeding ground" for terrorists (Williams et al, 2016; for further discussion on the discursive framing of Molenbeek and the impact on residents, see Ghalbzouri, 2018; Moderbacher, 2020). It is this dehumanizing discourse, exemplified in the statement by the French politician Éric Zemmour that "instead of bombing Raqqa, France should bomb Molenbeek" (Zemmour and Farge, 2015), that has enabled the violence directed toward communities living in these areas. Targeting Molenbeek as part of Plan Canal is thus an extension of the urban military operations launched in the cities in the Middle East, with shared racialized and colonial logic guiding warfare both inside and outside the metropolis.

Plan Canal became the central focus of the counterterrorism measures put in place by the Belgian Ministry of Security and Interior. For Jan Jambon, the Minister of Interior at the time, it became a flagship project; he made a public vow: "I'm going to clean up Molenbeek" (Jambon, 2015). This racial and masculinist assertion about "cleaning up" Molenbeek needs to be seen as part of the military logic of urban governance. If, in the words of Jan Jambon (2015), "we are at war with Islamic State," then Plan Canal is another extension of the colonial war-time logic that seeks to target and raid enemy territory. In other words, the state strategy articulated under Plan Canal operates under colonial logic as it seeks to assert control over a territory, rather than aiming to disable the specific criminal networks that facilitated the spate of indiscriminate killings in public spaces. As Achille Mbembe writes in the context of the European colonial expansion in Africa: "Colonial occupation itself was a matter of seizing, delimiting, and asserting control over a physical geographical area—of writing on the ground a new set of social and spatial relations" (2003: 25). This new set of socio-spatial relations is foregrounded in Plan Canal in the very imaginary of the city through a colonial wartime lens. Plan Canal is an example of the imaginative geographies that homogenize places and communities as a source of danger. Molenbeek and the area around the Canal are represented through orientalist spatial imaginaries as places of decay and naturalized violence that perpetually menace state power.

As noted by Heidi (this name is a pseudonym chosen by the participant, as are all the other participant names in the book), a long-term resident of Molenbeek, the presence of the police and the military in the neighborhood had an intense emotional impact on her and her neighbors. The police and military raids and stop and search in the neighborhood were, for her, disturbing to the point that she said these incidences were "much worse than the attacks itself."[1] Heidi was part of the long-standing working-class Italian immigration to this neighborhood, and she has seen it change drastically since the attacks. During our conversation, she recalled an event when special military forces raided an elementary school while she was there with the schoolchildren and other school personnel: "It was a lot of weapons, and the police were very aggressive," she recounted, and "it was a very scary, scary situation." The sight of weapons on the children's playground and the experience of confusion and panic, with children and their parents around, was traumatic for Heidi. It made a lasting impression on her; she was still reliving the experience at the time when I talked to her, almost four years after the event. She said that she still has "nightmares about this situation." She continued to wonder about the impact it has had on the young children that were present and all the parents and families involved.

For Heidi and her neighbors, the police and military presence and actions have heightened their experience of vulnerability and exposure to violence in their everyday surroundings. Thus, in Molenbeek, the presence of the military and the militarized police had a very different purpose than "reassuring citizens of their safety." In contrast, the military presence and soldiers instilled a sense of fear and uncertainty within a broad population, who found themselves viewed as potential threats. Indeed, western military doctrine has continuously emphasized the impossibility of distinguishing civilians from enemy combatants in situations of urban warfare, where enemies are imagined as "infiltrated" with, and indiscernible from, non-combatants (Amoore, 2009). This logic of conflating residents and enemies creates an imaginative geography of "a world where civilians do not exist" (Appadurai, 2006: 31). In this world, any injuries, suffering, and trauma of civilians is legitimized under the rubric of "collateral damage." The event that Heidi described underscores how this logic renders everybody as a potential target while at the same time destabilizing the notion of the "everyday" as a place outside the timespace of war. Geographies of everyday life are increasingly enmeshed with the logic of warfare, and the blurring of boundaries between enemies and civilians creates uncertainty and disorientation in the collective lifeworld in addition to suturing the possibility of threat and violence into an increasing range of mundane places and activities.

The mundane objects of the urban battlescape

In the aftermath of the attacks in Brussels, our discussions with law enforcement and municipal authorities revealed a notable sense of anxiety and unease characterizing their perception of the city as a place of danger. The prevailing discourse that an attack could occur at any moment and in any location led to the inclination to regard numerous seemingly innocuous objects as potential weapons and scrutinize mundane activities as suspicious behavior. One conspicuous example of these paranoid urban spatial imaginaries involved the implementation of a temporary lockdown on the morning of June 22, 2016, prompted by the report of a perceived terrorist threat. Several hours later, the security threat and the lockdown were lifted. Later in the day, we had an interview with a Brussels federal police officer who had happened to be tasked with assessing and managing this security "incident." During the interview, he told us, adding a touch of sarcastic humor to the story, that the cause of the alarm was a suspicious package discovered in a Brussels mall.[2] The officer explained to Sara Fregonese and me that a visibly mentally distraught man was being held as a terrorist suspect by Brussels police in one of the malls due to him possessing a suspicious bag of white powder. After securing the perimeter and imposing a temporary lockdown in the city, the police officers were carefully instructed to taste the white powder. They detected that it was sugar, not an explosive. Nevertheless, the police were further instructed to send the white powder to a lab for chemical analysis. According to the police officer supervising the "incident," only after the laboratory analysis substantiated the claims that it was indeed a bag of sugar could the security threat be said to be eliminated and the lockdown lifted.

The officer recounted this anecdote to highlight some of the absurdities that came up, but this episode also underscores the way a sense of imminent danger transformed the perception of mundane objects and behaviors in the city and heightened the need to enclose and fortify places deemed vulnerable. In the years that followed, the military logic of fortification and enclosure was gradually implemented in the very built environment of the city. In other words, as the military operations in the two cities were ending, and the presence of camouflaged soldiers was receding, the two cities witnessed a profound transformation of the infrastructural and material landscape. Both cities began to invest intensively in the process of shaping the everyday urban built environment as a defensive space used to mitigate threats. Borrowing mostly from military strategies (Graham, 2011), diffuse urban design elements were developed and put in place to fortify places deemed vulnerable. The integration of the logic of the battlefield into the everyday built environment is notably apparent in the widespread deployment of ubiquitous bollards on city streets (Figure 3.2). These devices serve to avert vehicular threats by preventing cars from colliding into buildings and pedestrians. The adoption of bollards underscores the transformation of city streets into environments where architectural elements serve as protective measures against potential threats, effectively blurring the traditional boundaries between civilian spaces and military operations in the everyday fabric of the city.

Indeed, the construction of such "security infrastructures" is one of the most important long-term counterterrorist measures in the two cities. Urbanists, planners, and architects, together with police officers, were tasked with devising and implementing an array of infrastructural solutions to fortify and protect the city. In Brussels, the city tasked the newly formed Bruxelles Prévention et Sécurité/Brussel Preventie en Veiligheid (Brussels Prevention and Security) office with the broad urban initiative of "designing-out terrorism."[3] Together with the Brussels Office for Urban Planning Perspective (perspective.brussels) and the Office for Urbanism (urban.brussels), they set out to form guidelines and lead projects to ensure security through the design of urban public spaces. As shown in Figure 3.3, the proposed solutions, besides bollards,

Figure 3.2: Bollards in Brussels, September 2019

Source: Author's own

included plants, benches, flowerpots, and lighting as elements of protective infrastructures.

The guiding logic behind these seemingly innocuous elements of the built environment is that in a situation where everything from a car to a sugar packet can be a weapon, equally, any object can serve as a protection device. Most of those measures were implemented in the so-called European quarter of Brussels, an affluent neighborhood that houses institutions and governing agencies of the EU (see Figure 3.2). The European quarter is thus represented as a space that needs protection and fortification, as it is perpetually under threat of violence stemming from individuals outside the area itself. Several features were also incorporated into the design of the pedestrian zone called *le piétonnier* around the Place de la Bourse, another flagship project of the city of Brussels. The development of security "hot-spots" around strategic

Figure 3.3: Excerpt from *Guide à l'intégration de dispositifs de sécurité dans l'espace public: Région de Bruxelles-Capitale* (2018)

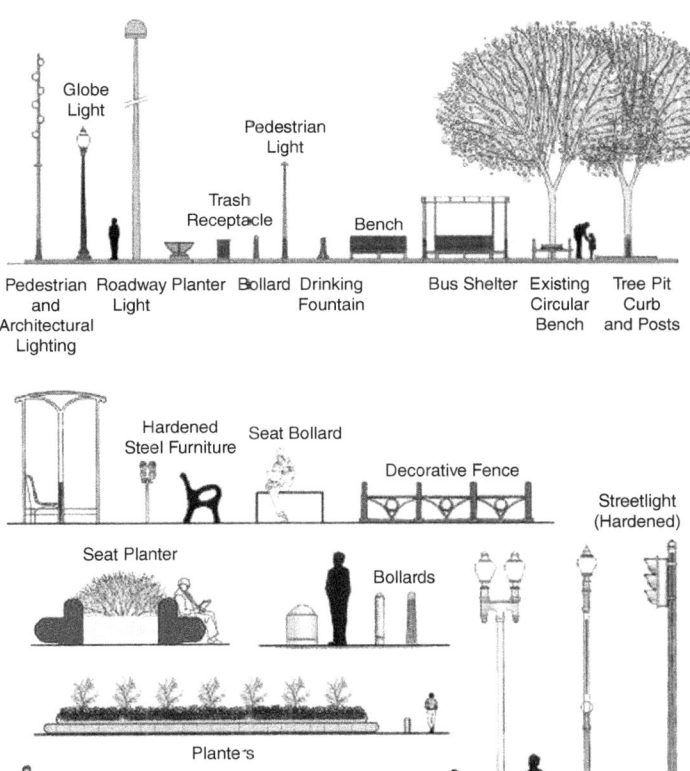

Note: The title for this part of the guide (not shown in the figure) reads: "Types of street furniture that, when properly sized, can play a role in making public spaces safer" (p 43).

Source: Perspective.Brussels (2018)

commercial, financial, and governmental centers echoes similar developments across many cities, from London's Ring of Steel to the gated communities across Africa, the Middle East, and Latin America.

In Paris, the Prefecture of the Police has had a department tasked with *prévention situationnelle* (situational prevention) since the early 1980s; the department is known as le Service opérationnel de prévention situationnelle. The purpose of the department, when it was initially set up, was prevention of burglaries and petty theft; the department went about this by setting up devices, such as video surveillance cameras, in urban public spaces or by introducing additional street lighting. According to an officer responsible for this department, the guiding idea behind their work in the management of urban public spaces and buildings is "the concept of to see and be seen."[4] He proceeded to explain to us the logic of visibility that they implement in urban spaces: "It is mainly to arrange the space so that there is no hidden corner." Visibility as the guiding concept in restructuring urban space to prevent unwanted behavior dates back even longer, however. It can be traced to the urban redevelopment of Paris under Baron Haussmann, a French official appointed by Napoleon III to be responsible for the large reconstruction of urban public spaces of Paris, predominantly to build large boulevards, in the second half of the 19th century. One of the guiding ideas behind Haussmann's construction of the big boulevards was to increase visibility in public space and, by doing so, decrease crime and theft (Mitchell, 1991; Ross, 2000). The new roads had a military function as well. The large boulevards were also intended to prevent the building of barricades and inhibit other forms of insurrectional activities and social unrest in the city, in addition to allowing military troops to enter the city if needed (Harvey, 2005).

Situational prevention can be seen as a continuation of the redesign of urban public spaces under military logic. This became especially evident following the attacks in 2015 when the police department for situational prevention became flooded with requests to reinforce the security of the city against the threat of terrorism.[5] Today, the prevention of terrorist activities is the department's primary function.

Similar to Brussels, their activities concentrate on setting up bollards and other anti-ramming devices, together with a host of other mundane "street furniture" intended for "hardening infrastructure." The purpose of these objects is, on the one hand, to deter a potential terrorist act in the location, and on the other hand, to reduce the anticipated impact of the potential attack. The logic behind the changes in urban spaces in anticipation of attack was further clarified by the police officer:

> Take for example a square. We say we don't want to put a fence around the square for the evening. We don't want to close it. However, what we recommend is ... we say ... for the time being, put the doors anyway, and you leave them open. But if something goes wrong, you can close them.

The fences around squares are thus linked to the logic of the door, rendering them part of the common-sense infrastructure in the city, where the idea of immutable openness is framed as inherently threatening and rationally unsound. Moreover, the building of fences and "doors" in urban public spaces is guided by the vision of the future of the city as a place of imminent violence. These elements of urban design thus work to imagine urban futures ridden with armed conflict and terrorist attacks, driving urban planning "for the war yet to come," in the words of Hiba Bou Akar (2018). Bou Akar writes in the context of Beirut's ongoing urbanization, describing the role of urban planning in the transformation of the city as guided by the logic of future war. She argues that these planning projects differ from the Haussmannian modernization interventions in cities insofar as they are lacking a vision for a better future and the promise of progress that once defined modernization projects. The future is no longer viewed as a guaranteed space of prosperity, but rather as uncertain or even perilous, marked by social fragmentation, instability, and violence. Dystopian visions and the management of urban public space, as described earlier, are driving similar logic in urban planning of (post)war cities in the global south. Across these cities, the orientation toward future war is shaping cities in the present, with the task for the urban built environment being to adapt to (future) crisis and preserve the status quo.

To help further theorizing in relation to war-torn cities, during my conversations with the members of the city government, planning officials, and the police, I often inquired about the transfer of knowledge that formed the basis of their activities and whether they drew on knowledge developed in traditional war contexts. Most of the time, the concrete transfer of knowledge was deemed confidential, and I was not given access to documents. Nevertheless, I often asked about the inspirations they drew from in their daily work so as to get a sense of how their activities situated in one city related to imaginative geographies of other cities and places. While the officer responsible for situational prevention in the city commented that they drew inspiration from Israel, among others, as a model of "best practices,"[6] he also quickly dismissed any association with warfare in the city, saying "we are not putting concrete walls everywhere, placing sandbags with shooters … or implementing checkpoints in Paris."

However, while the situational prevention department was not setting up checkpoints, another high-ranking officer responsible for public order in the city, who was based in La direction de l'ordre public et de la circulation (Public Order and Traffic Department), highlighted that one of the major changes in this department's daily work in the city following the attacks in 2015 involved the implementation of checkpoints. He commented: "I think we have shifted from an approach of public space which was an open approach, where public space is public by definition – so we can move freely – to an approach where we close, and we control." He proceeded to give the example of the pedestrianization of the Champs Elysées; at the time of the interview in January 2020, the street was turned into a pedestrian zone by the city once a month. The officer described the engagement of his unit in setting up an "anti-terrorist perimeter" in the area during these events, cordoning it off with anti-ram vehicles, and undertaking what he described as "filtering" of each person entering the Champs Elysées in addition to closing metros "so that our perimeter is not infiltrated by the interior, of course." He commented that these activities in everyday spaces and during mundane events were new for the police but that, at the same time, they were needed to keep the city safe. The officer further expounded on the changed relationship of the police toward public space, saying: "The population, the public space ... that is to say, a shared space ... is not completely public anymore, since it is controlled. There is limiting of movement, of the freedom to come and go."[7] This changed relationship to urban public space, especially within the city's public order department, is significant as it echoes critical urban scholarship that has celebrated, among other things, the possibility of anonymity in the city (Benjamin, 2023/1973) as crucial for political action and social emancipation. While the police officer spoke of a more controlled public space, it should be noted that for women and ethnic and racial minorities, public space in western cities has long been experienced as a controlled space, as feminist and other critical scholars have argued (Dikeç, 2013; Hancock and Mobillion, 2019; Najib, 2020).

The implementation of measures like checkpoints mirrors the logic of anti-terrorist lockdowns, emphasizing the need to enclose urban public spaces and regulate the movement of people within them. These measures, seemingly routine and mundane, are integrated into the fabric of everyday life in cities. Importantly, these mundane objects and activities in everyday spaces render the notion of urban warfare as a natural feature of life in the city. With checkpoints and restricted zones, we see a blurring of the lines between war zones and civilian places. The urban landscape itself becomes a reflection of the entangled relationship between war and everyday life, shaping how people, including city planning officials and police officers, perceive their environment and orient themselves within it. The mundane objects of the urban battlespace form an important way in which the notion of urban warfare is situated in place and in everyday life.

Urban redevelopment as banal warfare: the case of Brussels' Plan Canal

Besides setting up infrastructural changes and placing objects in public spaces based on the military logic of enclosure and fortification, the nexus between wars and the urban is also evident in projects of urban redevelopment. A poignant example of such a project is the aforementioned Plan Canal. As has been noted, the Ministry of Security and Interior initiated Plan Canal to enhance police and military presence in Molenbeek and other marginalized, racialized neighborhoods. In parallel with this security initiative, a redevelopment plan for the area, also known as the Plan Canal, was implemented. This strategy was launched already years prior by the regional government as part of the Brussels-Capital Region project, and it received significant additional investments after 2015. The intricate politics of the urban redevelopment aspect of the government's Plan Canal needs to be seen in light of the historic infrastructural development of this area. Specifically, the canal that runs along the north–south axis of the city was dug in the 19th century to serve as a transportation waterway connecting Brussels with other regions in the country. It was initially used for transportation of raw material, mostly coal, and gradually the canal helped inaugurate the intense period of industrialization of Brussels during the late 19th and early 20th centuries. Several industries started to develop around the Canal region in this period. This included chemical and petrochemical companies, gas and cement plants, warehouses, and logistics companies (canal.brussels, nd). The zone around the canal transformed also into a housing area for the families of workers who were increasingly coming to the city to work in the booming industry, which by the end of the 1960s employed around 160,000 people (canal.brussels, nd). At this time, Molenbeek and other municipalities along the canal became a welcoming area for so-called "guest workers" arriving in the city, mostly from southern Europe, Morocco, and Turkey but also from other French and Belgian former colonies. Starting in the 1970s, the area was affected by a process of severe deindustrialization when many factories closed, and more affluent residents started moving to the suburbs of the city. The area continued to provide housing for working-class residents, and today it remains a place where many migrants, refugees, and asylum seekers arrive (Meeus et al, 2019).

While the initial outline of the Plan Canal, as a program for "revitalizing" the former industrial area, had been presented by the regional government in 2013 (perspective.brussels, nd), major developments in Molenbeek started to become more visible after 2016. In short, under Plan Canal, the government has aimed to encourage investment of private capital into the area by renewing buildings and apartments to bring in more affluent residents. Private investors are incentivized to buy the cheap derelict buildings and other properties, renew them, and then sell them as luxury apartments. The new and booming housing market is presented by the government as a perfect investment opportunity, and it is supposed to attract the middle class that has been, until recently, avoiding this area. In addition to changing the housing market, Plan Canal has also brought the cultural industry to this area of the city. This side of the urban redevelopment project is exemplified by the building of the Museum of Modern Art and Centre Pompidou as well as the organizing of cultural events to bring tourists and cater to more affluent residents. The project is accompanied by an intense city marketing campaign to present the area as a trendy, hipster place that is being "reborn … from an industrial wasteland," in the words of the Brussels-Capital Region's tourism promotion and communications agency (visit. brussels, 2022). The vision of the area as a wasteland, which the initiative promotes, relies on the colonial trope of unoccupied territory and effectively conceals from view the citizens who have been living there for decades. This process of rendering invisible the citizens of Molenbeek is particularly evident in the recent proposal to build the Dockside Tower in the Canal area, a venture financed by the private real estate companies Urbicoon and Kumpen Real Estate. This much-publicized housing development proposes to build a 14-story tower to be used for housing, retail, and office space. The project is at the time of writing facing obstacles and some opposition from the local municipal government. One of the many issues that have been raised relates to the many one-bedroom apartments in the building, as that does not fit with the needs of existing residents in the area, which is marked by large population density and bigger family structures (van der Saag, 2023).

The process of gentrification presents itself as an indirect way of targeting the existing residents of these neighborhoods, which are stigmatized as a "Jihadi safe haven" (Gatti, 2019). In a conversation with Ibrahim, a long-time social worker and resident of the Canal area of Molenbeek, he brought up issues around gentrification as one of the most relevant changes in the neighborhood that exclude local working-class residents: "We initially thought it was going to create a local economy because a lot of people are going to come and work. But walou, nada, nothing at all!"[8] Ibrahim explained that many of the new businesses, from banks to museums and government offices, have catering facilities and restaurants inside their buildings. Effectively, the businesses, in his view, have barricaded themselves away from the surrounding neighborhood. He noted that "rather than going next door to eat at Moustapha's, at Antonio's, and so on, they open their own cafes and bakeries." In other words, the newly established businesses are purposefully constructed as inward-oriented, as if in a state of siege, rather than being open to their surroundings. Ibrahim remarked on many aspects of the material and economic fortressing associated with the buildings that have been refurbished for businesses and housing; these include the introduction of surveillance and security infrastructure and even the construction of buildings with windows facing the Bourse, on the other side of the canal, rather than the neighborhood itself. Moreover, he commented on the social fortressing, explaining that the new affluent residents rarely come or send their kids to the community center that he runs near the canal. For Ibrahim, these developments are a form of violence, one that is not direct, but rather demeaning and exclusionary. For him, it is another way of invalidating the working-class residents and not recognizing them as legitimate citizens.

The literature on conflict cities in the global south, predominantly those in the Middle East, has extensively documented how urban redevelopment initiatives, such as the processes of gentrification, entrench war geographies and the associated "us" versus "them" ideologies (Fawaz, 2009; Bou Akar, 2018; Genç, 2021; Rabie, 2021). The displacement of low- and middle-income families through capital-intensive housing development is often concentrated in places deemed as "trouble areas," or sources of instability in the city (Fawaz et al, 2012). The sectarian geographies are "played out over such issues as land and apartment sales, the occupation of ruins, access to housing, zoning and planning regulations, and infrastructure projects" (Bou Akar, 2018: 9). In times of peace, geopolitical conflict often operates through market mechanisms and economic strategies—processes taking place in the offices of bureaucrats and developers.

To summarize, in Brussels the government has taken a two-pronged approach in Plan Canal. On one hand, increased police presence and violent policing in the neighborhood create additional insecurities and anxieties, and on the other hand, urban redevelopment programs exacerbate and entrench existing inequalities. Even though the two aspects of Plan Canal originate from separate governing agencies that have different trajectories and, as such, appear seemingly unconnected, their operation is experienced as synergistic in creating further distrust, fear, and exclusion. Gentrification is then a logical extension of the need to "clean up" Molenbeek, by displacing its current residents, and to reclaim the "enemy territory," through the occupation of space by private capital. What is more, the question of urban planning and redevelopment brings to the forefront that the notion of urban war is not simply an instrument of the state or the military, but dispersed across a range of different actors, including for-profit developers, real estate agents, and cultural industry corporations, thus embedding the notion of urban warfare, and associated notions of xenophobia and exclusion, deep within the circuits of global capital.

Performativity of warfare in the city

While lockdown and state of emergency are time-delimited measures, this chapter has addressed how the notion of warfare has become a more durable condition of the urban, well beyond temporal emergencies. Discourses and practices of warfare are not tied to specific events, crises, and violent emergencies in the two cities; they also frame urban governance in the long term. Specifically, warfare rationalities underly the transformations in the very urban built environment that the city governments have embarked on in recent years, emphasizing the interconnectedness of warfare discourses and the physical urban landscape. The process of shaping urban landscapes as battlescapes (Graham, 2006) began with the presence of camouflaged soldiers on city streets and was followed by the gradual replacement of military bodies with the proliferation of bollards, anti-ramming devices, and other efforts for "designing out terrorism" (Coaffee, 2004). In contrast to the more visible enactments of urban warfare, such as the military and heavily armed police on the streets and squares and the presence of military-grade equipment, these elements of the built environment are more innocuous "flaggings" or reminders of urban threat. These objects, while they may go unnoticed, nevertheless have significant political agency on their own since they *create an effect* of ongoing warfare as they are repeatedly encountered in daily life. They bring into being or, in other words, performatively enact the notion of permanent warfare. It is their routinized incorporation into daily practices that stabilizes the sense of threat and the associated war geographies. These "everyday, routinized, barely noticed reminders" (Katz, 2007: 350) exemplify the performativity of security in everyday spaces that works to normalize militarism and conflict. Rather than purportedly protecting and defending the city, these performative bodies and objects are repetitive enactments that constitute and stabilize the process of making war present in the city in ways that collapse the distinction between everyday civilian spaces and military space. Moreover, the performativity of warfare in the city shapes the ongoing orientation toward anticipated crisis; it materializes in the present the potentiality of future warfare.

Importantly, in terms of theorizing with war-torn cities, the security mechanisms can be seen to be "building territories, entrenching enclaves, and solidifying divisions in the city" (Fawaz et al, 2012: 190). The narratives of warfare that rely on the nationalist and xenophobic discourse of "us" and "them" also shape the imaginary geographies of the city as a Manichean space dichotomized according to the vulnerable city and the enemy territory. In the context of the vulnerable city, these elements of the urban landscape serve as visual reminders of the protective state, intended to reassure the good citizen and deter the unwanted behavior, including terrorist attacks, of the bad citizen. In the context of the enemy territory, performativities of warfare are put in place to occupy and eliminate the threatening "other" as well as to create the effect of confluence between supposedly indistinguishable enemies and civilians.

The chapter used the example of Plan Canal and its implementation in the neighborhood of Molenbeek as a synergistic government activity connecting increased military and police presence with the urban redevelopment of the area.

In doing so, the chapter underscored the violent implications of architecture and urban planning (Weizman, 2007; Pullan, 2011) and projects of urban redevelopment (Fawaz, 2009; Bou Akar, 2018). Here, we see an intertwining of private market and state interventions as they enact war geographies, with the same military logic of containment and exclusion being embedded within shopping centers and housing developments. The stories of Heidi and Ibrahim and the residents of the neighborhood showed how the material and infrastructural changes have profoundly affected their sense of place. More than time-delimited events or mundane changes, these practices and government initiatives have transformed their emotional relationship to their everyday environment, either through an increased sense of vulnerability or through experiences of exclusion in the neighborhood. The next chapter turns to the processes of reassembling the embodied, the affective, and the sensorial in cities of banal warfare.

FOUR

Affective Atmospheres "on the Front Line"

The following is an excerpt from a conversation with Marco, a high-ranking officer working for la Direction de l'ordre public et de la circulation (the Department of Public Order and Traffic) at the Préfecture de Police (Prefecture of Police) in Paris in October 2021.

Marco: The events in 2015 have deeply impacted the way we do our work as police officers. For a start, it is our equipment. I will give you a simple example of a semi-automatic rifle, which is a military-grade weapon: if you would have dared to propose it before 2015, everyone would have said that France is not at war! Now this is part of our standard equipment.

Sunčana: What else has changed in your daily work?

Marco: Well besides the revolution in the use of weapons and in the procedures we follow, there has been a real philosophical change inside the heads of police officers. Now we realize we can be a target! For example, I'm going on a vacation with my family a week from now, and I will take my weapon with me! Before, we would leave our weapons in the office; now almost all police officers keep the weapons even when they are off duty. Because

> it can happen as you go grocery shopping, for example, and there's a shooter and you don't have a bulletproof vest. It can happen in supermarkets, theatre halls ... but I tell you that it is extremely difficult. There is this awareness, but also the tension and willpower. But it can be tiring, as you say yourself, madam. My wife often makes fun of me because the first thing I do in a store is to take a look at the entrance or the emergency exit in the store and what the atmosphere is like in any store. Many of my colleagues, many policemen do this. We are spotted in the stores because what we do is we take a little look.[1]

This lengthy excerpt provides an insight into the affective dynamics of urban warfare in the city of Paris. Here, the notion "we are at war" translates into a host of embodied, sensorial, and perceptual changes in everyday life, developments Marco calls "philosophical changes" in police officers' mind (in his words, "changement philosophique dans la tête des policiers"). The following section addresses these philosophical changes by situating them within the concept of affective atmospheres, specifically regarding the changed ambiance and atmospheric sense of place in the city. The chapter addresses the politics of affect that shapes urban atmospheres and explores how such atmospheric relations are crucial for reinstating dominant understandings of urban warfare.

Orchestrating atmospheres of vigilance

To gain a deeper insight into Marco's account of the changes in his daily life, both on and off duty, it is worth taking a closer look at how the state has articulated understanding of urban conflict, violence, and crisis and the way to respond to this. As addressed earlier, state discourses and practices have continuously articulated the notion of permanent warfare, where an attack can happen anytime, anywhere. As Marco says, an attack could take place when you go grocery shopping or go out to a theater, or when you are on vacation. The question of how one responds to permanent urban warfare is evident already in the name of the aforementioned Opération Sentinelle (Operation Sentinel). The word *sentinelle* has multiple meanings in French: it can mean a soldier on guard or it can mean a watchtower. The word stems from the Latin *sentiō* or the Italian *sentire*, and it means to feel, hear, smell, and perceive with the senses. A *sentinelle* is, then, a person who is tasked to employ all their senses to guard and protect as well as notify others in case of perceived danger. L'opération Sentinelle is part of the French Plan Vigipirate, a government security alert program that has long relied on the framework of vigilance to formulate the state's response to the notion of permanent warfare. According to the Prefecture de Police website, Plan Vigipirate is "one of the permanent tools of the global fight against terrorism: it involves all the players (state, local authorities, public and private operators, and citizens) in an approach based on vigilance, prevention, and protection" (Prefecture de Police, nd; own translation). Vigilance is a form of embodiment organized, managed, and sustained by formal state and non-state actors as a key framework of military urbanism. It signifies heightened alertness and continuous watchfulness for the danger permanently present across urban spaces.

Through the state-cultivated framework of vigilance, we can understand the philosophical changes that Marco mentioned are now part of their job. Marco referred to feelings of tension and resilience but also an intense awareness of his fragility as a "target" of the "enemy." These feelings seem to accompany him, and his colleagues, everywhere they go. I would argue these are not simply individually experienced emotions, but socially produced and relationally shared affective atmospheres of vigilance that envelope places in Marco's daily life.[2] The seeming inability to retreat from warfare further showcases these affective geographies of vigilance, with Marco and his colleagues carrying their weapons when in their homes, while doing their daily errands, and even on vacation. The affective atmospheres of vigilance are thus put "on the front line" of the "war against terror," with significant consequences. For example, France has recorded a continuously increasing number of suicides among members of the police force (Le Monde, 2019). Moreover, although the data is inconclusive, police officers suffer to a greater extent from anxiety and depression (Bénézit, 2022). These issues are arguably partly due to the taxing psychological weight of permanent warfare.

Marco also described how this affective state of vigilance felt and how it was embodied in his daily life. Discussing his behavior in supermarkets, he mentioned a reliance on visual scanning (in his words, "*jette des coups d'œil*"—literally, throw an eye) of his surroundings. He would further seek to orient himself in space, paying attention to the spatial layout. And, finally, he would try to assess and sense "*l'ambiance*" (the atmosphere). The conversation delved further into the elusive ways he would sense the atmosphere in a store. He described how he would try to "detect" something strange and out of the ordinary in a place, since for him a terrorist threat is "*protéiforme et diffuse*" (protean and diffuse). A complex application of the senses is required to control a threat that is seemingly elusively dispersed across different geographies. Marco's experiences echo a rise of the discourses and practices of vigilance to construct "resilience" to combat urban terrorism. Many countries, as part of the state engineering of vigilance, are going beyond the significant reliance on the visual (this reliance is exemplified in the If You See Something, Say Something campaign employed in cities across Europe and the United States to enhance vigilance; Amoore, 2007; Arfsten, 2019). These countries seek to apply the sensorial and phenomenological underpinnings of vigilance. In other words, vigilance, or so-called "situational awareness" (Krasmann and

Hentschel, 2019), involves not only detecting what "looks out of place," but also what feels out of place. Here, we see an example of the way urban warfare is not merely produced and reproduced through legal documents, state and media discourses, military equipment, and technologies, but seeps deep into bodily senses and bodily orientations in the city, in ways that are difficult to grasp and often unquestioned. Rather than simply being individual experiences, the affective atmospheres of vigilance are constructed in relation to human bodies, urban built environment, discourses, objects, and materials that reiterate, often unconsciously, the military logic of life in the city.

Police and the affective presencing of warfare

During our conversations with police responsible for maintaining public order in the city, warfare was a recurring theme. Warfare was more than materially present in the equipment they used, or "the revolution in the use of weapons," to use Marco's words; he was referring mostly to the G36— an automatic rifle, made by German weapons manufacturer Heckler & Koch, that is commonly used in war; warfare was also intensely embodied and affectively present in day-to-day police work.

Benoit, a police officer working as part of Paris' compagnie d'intervention (intervention unit), was responsible for policing public demonstrations as well as festive and sports events in the city. He joined this task force after coming to Paris from the provinces; he had seen television reports on the so-called "yellow vest" protests in the city and decided to "come here and help my colleagues [*camarades*]."[3] Benoit portrayed the public demonstrations in Paris as an act of war, and, like Marco, he identified himself and his fellow officers as targets. However, for Benoit, the declaration of warfare comes not from the figure of the "terrorist," but from the figure of the "*casseur*," a pejorative term for a demonstrator who tries to "*casser le flic*" (break the cop). He described the process of getting ready for maintaining public order during demonstrations as preparation for entering the battlefield. He said: "we go up to the maximum level, with the hood, helmet, protective glasses, we have a gas mask, protections for the shoulders, protections for the arms, for the legs, a shell for the genitals if we take a projectile on it"; he was always reminding his colleagues that "you have to be hyper-attentive, hyper-vigilant every day." Vigilance thus formed an important affective orienting device in his daily life.

Moreover, Benoit's office was filled with mundane objects he had taken from the "*casseurs*" (rioters) as artifacts to remind him that the demonstrators are enemies always ready to attack the police. This constant reminder of the ongoing warfare kept him on alert during his missions. This affective presencing, or making present, of warfare in his workspace or as he patrolled the city streets also significantly shaped Benoit's subjectivity. He commented that "an intervention unit officer is the traditional officer for maintaining order and, as we say sometimes, he is a soldier. We ask him to have a shield, to hold a position." In other words, Benoit saw himself and his colleagues as soldiers as he situated his subjectivity with respect to the affective atmospheres of urban warfare. Further on in the conversation, Benoit began to address questions of mental health in his unit, openly discussing police suicide. Like Marco, he attributed the poor mental health among police officers to the fatigue of having to be on maximum alert and always watchful of the enemy, adding: "Luckily it's not every day there's a war."

Our exchange with Benoit underscores how the framework of warfare not only shape perceptions of incidents, which may be labeled as terrorist acts attributed to racialized Muslims and immigrants, but also influence the interpretation of other events categorized as disruptions to public order within the urban landscape, including public demonstrations. While some police officers commented that the anti-terrorist equipment used during public demonstrations was there to "protect the protesters" in case of an impending outsider attack,[4] other members of the police were quite critical of what they saw as a confluence of the notion of terrorist with the notion of demonstrator. One of the critics, Ismail, an officer working at the Préfecture de Police in Paris, noted a change in the discourse within the police approach to demonstrators, with some of the higher-ranking officers often referring to "*connards*", a degrading expression meaning jerks.[5] During our conversation, he further mentioned the dangerous move toward "confusing terrorists with *casseurs*" to justify the increasingly repressive ways of policing that he had observed. He mentioned the use of heavy weapons and "anti-terrorist" devices during demonstrations in the city and said that he had observed the public's fears that the police would use these "anti-terrorist" devices against the demonstrators. For him, this represented a shift in the method of policing, maintaining a "war atmosphere." It should be noted however, as Matthieu Rigouste (2017) reminds us, that these developments need to be seen along the historical continuum of French policing, which has for decades regularly relied on military practices and equipment for "maintaining order" in racialized, working-class neighborhoods in the city.[6]

Recruiting citizen-soldiers

As noted earlier, within Plan Vigipirate, it is not only police, military, and other official state actors that are responsible for detecting threats and acting as a "*sentinelle*" (sentinel). Indeed, the program also heavily emphasizes the recruitment of citizens and individuals into the governing framework of vigilance. This reliance on citizens' state of vigilance is addressed through government-organized training programs for citizens, brochures that instruct citizens on how to be alert and watchful in different places (such as malls, concert halls, and supermarkets), and finally through banal daily reminders in the form of stickers or audio announcements throughout the different spaces of the city. During our conversations with police, the issue of citizens' enrolment into the vigilance framework was often brought up. Some police officers were adamantly against the project of creating watchful citizens, saying that this was the job of the police and that it should remain that way.[7] Others demanded more investment by citizens in the vigilance framework.

Claude, for example, a long-time police officer responsible for "situational prevention" in Paris, found problematic what he saw as the tendency of citizens to be inattentive, commenting that "the French have a kind of Latin tendency; we are less disciplined than others. Security requires rigor. That's a state of mind."[8] Marco, the police officer mentioned earlier, similarly compared his fellow citizens to those in other nations and bemoaned their lack of preparedness, which he saw as creating additional stress and responsibility for the police. Marco specifically compared French citizens with Israeli citizens as he was discussing how there are fewer "terrorist knife attacks" in Israeli cities; he explained: "there's always either an armed citizen who neutralizes it, and people carry emergency medical kits, they're trained in first aid and so on ... so they are a society that participates in security. In France, this is absolutely not the case!"[9] Both Claude and Marco thus acknowledged the relevance of the project of recruiting citizen-soldiers as subjectivities that require a specific form of embodiment, such as a "mindset" oriented towards watchfulness, discipline, and preparedness. It is, therefore, necessary to further zoom into these everyday affective geographies of residents to question the everyday embodiment of the affective state of vigilance and to address how these forms of embodiment are involved in the doing or undoing of urban warfare.

During walk-alongs in the 10th arrondissement with Eric, a middle-aged man who had been living in Paris for ten years,[10] the state project of creating watchful citizens (see also Ochs, 2011) was particularly pertinent to the discussion. When we discussed his experiences of discomfort in the city, he would bring up memories of living in his home country, before coming to Paris. Eric explained that he had lived most of his life in a place of long-time intermittent warfare, where bombings, attacks, and civilian casualties were recurring events. During the attacks in 2015 in Paris, Eric's embodied memories of past events resurfaced within his new urban surroundings, and this previous experience of violence provided him with a sense of security in his ability to navigate the urban violence. He half-jokingly commented that he had never thought his previous experiences would be useful in his Parisian life, but now he felt thankful for his experiences of warfare and terrorism.

Eric's comments demonstrate how the discourses on warfare that were circulated with the attacks in 2015 and 2016 also impacted residents' embodied and intimate understanding of these events as acts of warfare. In the years following the attacks, Eric continued to find this form of embodied knowledge of warfare to be useful in his daily life in the city. Specifically, he considered it an advantage to have lived before in a place of low-intensity warfare since it gave him a crucial edge to be able to spot and react to suspicious behavior. As we walked around the city, Eric described in detail the activities he would engage in to detect threat (for example, watching for sudden movements), the attention he would give to specific objects (for example, noticing objects that are out of place in the city), and the adjustments he would undertake to mitigate potential dangers (for example, avoiding overcrowded spots and dark areas). He was proud of his watchful orientation and, moreover, he considered it his duty to keep this up to protect himself and his family. He also commented on what he saw as the careless and nonchalant mindset of his fellow Parisians, who seemingly did not stay alert to such dangers. Therefore, for Eric, watchfulness was not only a vital part of his urban life but also a trait of a good citizen.

The state orchestration of vigilance is not exclusive to Paris, but forms part of the affective register of counterterrorism activities in many other European cities where we witness the responsibility for detecting threats being placed at the level of the individual. The affectivities of vigilance are also spatial phenomena that operate alongside imaginative geographies of safety and threat in the city. During walk-alongs in Brussels, participants often used vigilance as a dominant experiential framework for making sense of and positioning themselves in relation to urban areas that are stigmatized as "terrorist safe havens." It was for these reasons that some residents of Brussels told us they seek to avoid certain areas of the city, predominantly the municipality of Molenbeek and the Canal area, but also the Place de la Bourse, which sits adjacent to the Canal area. One of these residents was Emma, who I met for a walk-along on the Place de la Bourse one late afternoon in summer 2023. This is a time when the square typically comes alive, filled with the sounds of friends meeting up and music playing, however Emma quickly told me that she would prefer that we did not stay around the square during our walk together. She suggested that we walk away from the square and towards the eastern side of the city, where she felt more comfortable.[11] Emma had been living and working in the European quarter of Brussels for five years and she felt extremely unsafe in the city. She told me that her flat had been broken into and that she had been mugged on the street during her time in Brussels. Aside from crime-related issues, Emma felt acutely vulnerable to possible armed attacks in many everyday situations, even though she had not been living in Brussels during the attacks in 2015 and 2016. "When I hear somebody shout, I immediately think it is an attack," she said, adding: "Even when I see someone running, I think there might be an attack happening." These rather mundane sights and sounds were experienced by Emma as alerts to possible danger. In contrast to Eric, who saw his orientation towards potential danger as bolstering his sense of security and command over unruly urban threats, Emma found this to be intensely emotionally exhausting. She watched out for car attacks in crowds, knife attacks in public spaces, and possible muggings in the metro and on the streets, saying that "at any moment I think somebody might start breaking things, killing, or just going crazy." She reported never having felt like this before, even though she had "previously lived in other big European metropolises" Molenbeek and the area around the canal (Figure 4.1) made Emma particularly uncomfortable and she sought to avoid them altogether.

When I asked Emma if she had had any bad experiences there, she told me that she had gone to Molenbeek by accident once and had felt acutely unsafe. She had felt as though everybody was looking at her, which made her pay attention to the way she looked, how she acted, and the clothes she wore. It was at that moment that Emma told me that she is a Muslim but she does not look and behave like the people she identified as fellow Muslims in Molenbeek. Here, questions of racial, gendered, and classed subjectivity come to the fore, with Emma feeling out of place and under threat in this area of the city. Responding to the city's campaign, as part of Plan Canal, to entice more affluent residents to this area, Emma retorted: "I wouldn't live near the canal even if it was gratis!" Similarly, Emma told me she had heard of several stores in Molenbeek that sell groceries from her home country that are unavailable in other areas of the city, yet she did not feel safe visiting these stores. Even though Emma had experienced direct violence, such as muggings and burglaries, in other areas of the city, it was the area around the canal and Molenbeek that she tried to avoid altogether. This feeling of insecurity, she said, was widely shared among her colleagues and friends in the city.

To sum up, in cities of banal warfare, we see how both official state actors, such as police, and non-state actors, such as residents, are recruited into the affective state of vigilance in the city. For some, the sensorial orientation toward potential threat and embodied watchfulness for anticipated danger provides a sense of mastery and control over these sorts of event, which could seemingly happen anytime, anywhere. For others, the affective urban atmospheres exacerbate their feelings of vulnerability in the ongoing warfare and, as such,

Figure 4.1: The Canal area of Brussels on the border of Molenbeek, July 2023

Source: Author's own

are extremely emotionally taxing. In either case, these forms of embodiment continue to reproduce the notion of urban warfare in everyday urban environments and continuously strengthen the military logic of control and defense.

Countering radicalization as psychological warfare

Besides vigilance, another key affective domain of state-orchestrated counterterrorism is the so-called de-radicalization. In recent years, de-radicalization has burgeoned into an important and widespread state strategy for countering terrorism (Alloul, 2019; Jaminé and Fadil, 2019; Nguyen, 2019). The discourse of radicalization has gained prominence as an "empty signifier" to fight "the homegrown terrorist" in diverse settings, ranging from the US' Countering Violent Extremism task force and the UK's Prevent strategy to China's policing of the Uyghur population. It has also become a central strategy of Belgium's counterterror response since the events in 2015 as the discourse of the "enemy within" has increasingly gained prominence. Indeed, in my conversation with Ifeta, a city government representative in a Brussels municipality, radicalization was brought up as one of the most important security concerns in the years following the attacks.[12] "We are told that Syria is over, and it is supposed to be reassuring. But we are not [reassured]!" Ifeta said, "because we have [in Brussels] more and more people who are radicalized in schools … that's the new generation of radicalized people and their aim is not Syria." She went on to describe how the city government was surprised when they found out that the perpetrators of the Paris attack were from Brussels: "We were at the time [of the attacks in Paris] far from thinking that those people go to our schools rather than coming from immigration." Here, Ifeta set out an opposition between nation-state citizens and non-citizens ("immigrants"), saying that violence was usually associated with those coming from the outside. But, unable to hold that opposition in place, Ifeta's account of the events turned inward in an enactment of the military logic of the "enemy within," rather than using the logic of an external enemy of the state and the nation. For Ifeta, the security concerns clustered around the neighborhood of Molenbeek; she asked rhetorically: "How come there are some neighborhoods in Brussels where we had a community protecting the bad guy?" This "community" was referred to later in our conversations as the poor and Muslim residents of Brussels who feel, in Ifeta's words, "frustrated." Their "frustration," she said, comes from living close to the center of the city, as in the case of Molenbeek. Comparing this area to the urban geographies of Paris, she noted:

> In Paris, usually the poor people live on the margins of the city, the banlieues. In Brussels, it is a bit contrary to that. They are in the city itself. So even though they would be the poorest, they would go to the same schools as you and I. And that's where the frustration [in Brussels] comes from. And they are just under our view, living the same lives as us!

In short, Ifeta continued to set out an opposition between "us" (non-violent nation-state citizens, inviting the author into her definition of "us") and "them" (poor and frustrated residents). However, the difference between us and them was, for Ifeta, difficult to detect: "they live the same lives as us" and "go to the same schools as you and me." And this is where she saw the danger since, as she explained, it is difficult to identify and target the "others" as perpetrators of violence as they are living "just under our view." For the city government, this is a continuous source of anxiety in the ongoing warfare. The enemy is an invisible yet constantly present threat.[13]

It was for these reasons that the city and this municipality undertook major initiatives in the aftermath of the Paris and Brussels attacks. First, for tourism purposes, the city aimed to recover its "image" in the international media. To counter the image of Brussels as a place of danger and warfare, the city government introduced an intense marketing campaign to "rebrand." An important aspect of the city government strategy, according to Ifeta, was to create distance from the image of Molenbeek: "We needed to break that image: Molenbeek is not representative of the region. Sorry, sorry, but it's 1 municipality;

there are 18 others." In addition to the marketing campaign, another important city-wide initiative was to establish a de-radicalization program on the level of the municipality. Each of the 19 municipalities in Brussels is equipped with its own de-radicalization "cell," with further de-radicalization programs assembled at the federal and regional levels.

These programs are an odd mix of social work and psychological counseling combined with militaristic language—for example, the de-radicalization teams are called "pre-rad cells." They aim to identify and target residents even *before* they start to plan an act of political violence, opening up the space of the pre-crime as a site of potential state security intervention (Heath-Kelly, 2017). What is interesting to note here is that the space of the pre-crime is identified entirely in psychological terms as "a process in which an individual or a group *psychologically prepares* to commit acts of violence in the name of an ideology" (Bravvo, nd; own translation, emphasis added). Lucas, an official working in one of the many "de-radicalization cells" in the city, further defined violent radicalization as "a cognitive and behavioral change"; this emphasizes that the dominant views on human behavior, including political violence, employed psychological terms. Throughout our conversation, Lucas used many expressions from conventional psychology, such as when he spoke about the individual's "psychosocial vulnerability" to violent extremism and the cell's task of "reinforcing resilience" of individuals and groups affected by violent extremism.[14] Here, the mind and the body are set up as primary sites for identifying "the phenomenon" of violent radicalization as well as crucial sites of intervention for "diffusing" violent tendencies (see also Younis, 2021). While Lucas did not specify the "cognitive and behavioral changes" that form part of the process of violent radicalization, the city website was more specific in the communication with the public, providing a list of behaviors or "indicators" "*à quoi il faut être attentive*" (to watch out for). However, the list is still vague and points to quite mundane behaviors:

> The individual gradually changes his or her behavior, appearance, values, and discourse in line with a particular political or religious identity. The person ceases activities and hobbies previously practiced and distances him/herself from long-standing friends. He or she regularly frequents social networks, forums, or people claiming the same identity as him or her. The person increasingly expresses anger, frustration, and a sense of injustice, particularly towards the state, democratic institutions, and values. (Bravvo, nd; own translation)

As with vigilance, in de-radicalization programs, we observe this turn toward scrutinizing mundane behaviors and enforcing state control of the intimate spaces and bodies of people who are suspected of becoming the enemy. These strategies find their roots in the psychological dimensions of warfare, such as the military tactics of "winning hearts and minds," but this time they are deployed on the "home front" to combat the "enemy within."

While Lucas was adamant that the "phenomenon" of violent radicalization does not discriminate on the basis of religion and race, but rather considers everyone as a potential suspect, other officials working in the de-racialization cells are increasingly critical of these policies as they target Muslim and other urban residents that are racialized as "immigrants" or "foreigners." One of these officials, Iris, thought that the cell's engagement in prevention under the umbrella of de-radicalization is stigmatizing and unjust; she said: "You cannot target a group that has nothing to do with terrorism and say they *might* radicalize one day. Based on which criteria!? Because they are poor? Because they are of foreign origin [*allochtone*]?!"[15] Iris here echoed that the discourse of violent radicalization relies on a racialized construct as it refers to people who are anticipated to be dangerous rather than known to be dangerous. This anticipation, or suspicion, is not a scientifically neutral or objective assessment as some of the policies on violent radicalization claim. Rather, it has historic, political, and racialized underpinnings, with some bodies and communities more readily identified as enemies and terrorists than others. For Sara Ahmed, "the word terrorist sticks to some bodies as it reopens past histories of naming, just as it slides into other words" (2004: 131). Suspicion as an affective register sticks to bodies that are anticipated to be dangerous rather than known as being dangerous (see also Puar, 2018/2007). The anticipation is historically situated through repetitive framing of Muslim, Black, and migrant bodies as dangerous and abject, creating racialized atmospheres of suspicion in the city.

Recasting the enemy

Vigilance, suspicion, and radicalization all form the anticipatory regimes of the governance of terrorism. These regimes, moreover, work on the level of affective atmospheres to recast the subjectivities of those who are anticipated to be enemies.[16] This became particularly evident during walk-alongs with people in the two cities who have been differently affected by the racializing regimes of vigilance and radicalization. A research assistant and I met one of these people, Daniel, at the square of the Place de la République on a rainy day in late August 2020. At the time, the country was still under a health state of emergency, but restrictions on movement in the city were significantly reduced. Just a few months earlier, Parisians had been banned from leaving their homes; if they needed to go outside, they had to fill out a form to state why, and then when they were outside, they could only move within a one-kilometer radius of their home (Boulakia and Mariot, 2023). At the time of the interview, mask-wearing was mandatory in all public spaces in the city, including parks, streets, and squares (Figure 4.2).

Daniel, who was in his fifties, had lived in Paris all his adult life. He had been coming to the Place de la République almost daily for the past couple of years. He organized informal dance

Figure 4.2: Masks and security infrastructure on the square at the Place de la République, August 2020

Source: Author's own

get-togethers on the square, which brought in a diverse crowd of people almost every evening. From passers-by to more regular participants, all would move to the rhythms of salsa, bachata, traditional dances, and many others. On a rainy day like the one of the interview, however, the outdoor dancing on the square was cancelled. Daniel had experienced many changes on the square in recent years, including numerous public protests and demonstrations, the ban on public gatherings following the declaration of a state of emergency in 2015, and, at the time of the interview, the restrictions on movement related to the health state of emergency and the mandatory mask-wearing. For Daniel,

> they [politicians] are creating a war between people. ... They used the attacks, now they use COVID; it's the same, right? Next year they're going to use something else. COVID is an attack [*attentat*] for me, but it's a global attack. It's not an attack in Paris anymore or whatever; it's a global attack [*attentat mondial*].

Daniel drew connections between the seemingly disparate events that had been reverberating on the square and in his daily life in the past years. He recognized and challenged the narratives of warfare, and said that, for him, "*c'est encore politique*" (it's still politics).

Reflecting on the feelings of discomfort that he observed on or around the square, Daniel commented that he experienced that other people felt insecure or threatened by his presence in a public space. "*Je suis noir moi*" (I am Black), he stated. "So if I'm walking down the street, I'm going to run into someone, the person is going to change sidewalk or cover their pocket. So I feel like I make people feel insecure, you know what I mean." Daniel was bothered by people perceiving him as a threat on account of his dark skin and blamed Right-wing politicians for the atmosphere of distrust and racism. "I feel insecure [*Je me sens en insécurité*] because of all those who are afraid of Black people," he said. When I asked him if that affected his behavior in the city, he commented that he "is not going to wear a tie to please [*pour faire plaisir*]." Daniel was attuned to other people's perception of him in the city, and he directed his attention to notice, almost daily, other people's subtle body movements when around him (for example, crossing to a different side of the street and shielding their pockets). His attentiveness to other people's watchfulness in his presence created a somewhat different form of embodiment of the affective geographies of vigilance than that discussed previously in relation to Marco.

The narratives of urban warfare have heavily relied on nationalistic discourse posing divisions and constructing the notion of the "enemy within" by weaponizing racial, ethnic, and religious differences. The affective atmospheres of vigilance, radicalization, and suspicion, thus, redraw boundaries between communities, shaping atmospheric walls and other atmospheric materialities of enclosure, further evident in (post-)conflict cities elsewhere (Laketa, 2024). The atmospheric barriers are real and tangible "things" that determine who belongs and who does not belong, who feels at home and who feels out of place, and as such affective atmospheres engage in the processes of construction and reconstruction of subjectivites. The reproduced antagonisms, and any challenge to them, are thus much more insidious and less visible, and hence difficult to grasp. These atmospheres further performatively recast the notion of the "enemy within." "Others," such as migrants, Black people, and Muslims, are not only excluded from the polity but also represented as the enemy that is permanently and structurally embedded as a threat within the unruly spaces of the city.

Daniel was also aware of ways he might reduce the tension during his daily encounters, which included changing his bodily appearance to appear nonthreatening to others (such as wearing a tie to signify the civilized and not dangerous "European"). However, he refused to transform his body in that way to assuage fears and reduce discomfort ("*pour faire plaisir*"). In other words, Daniel was engaged in the affective geographies of vigilance, though not to "detect the enemy," but rather to help him negotiate the spaces of the city where he was perceived as a threat.

War atmospherics

This chapter addressed some of the main affective and experiential properties of living in cities of banal warfare, paying particular attention to state politics of affect. These elements form an important layer in shaping atmospheric relations, together with the physical elements of the urban environment and the discursive and media landscape, discussed in Chapters 2 and 3. Taken together, the discursive, the material, and the affective are processually assembled and reassembled in (re)creating war atmospherics. In that sense, war atmospherics make up a loose constellation that at times materializes and coagulates into a fixed "thing", shaping places and subjectivities in the city. The multiple forces at play in creating war atmospherics point to a more intangible register of power. Power, here, is not simply confrontational, although the potential for confrontation, coercion, and violence retains a palpable presence. Rather, relations of power are understood as a process of making some choices or some orientations more readily available. The process is not predetermined, however, as atmospheric relations are never fixed, but constantly reassembled through daily habitual practices in ways that are fluid and porous.

Atmospheric properties of war have been discussed in many conflict cities and places. In these places, violence is experienced "as a chronic, lingering intensity, an immense ethereal concentration" (Aijazi, 2024: 6), with attention turned to felt, visceral, and sensed contours of space. In places like East Jerusalem and occupied Palestine, the violence of the occupation operates not just through physical force but also through sounds, sights, and sensory experiences that shape political belonging and exclusion. Nadera Shalhoub-Kevorkian (2017) highlights how the violence of occupation extends to embodied experiences and atmospheric relations in ways that reinforce the state political project of settler colonialism. Similarly, in Egypt under President Sisi, control of the soundscape became a key element in consolidating state power (Malmström, 2019). Sounds, or the suppression of them, became a tool for maintaining political authority. Atmospheric relations themselves can also be violent and toxic, shaping inhospitable and harmful environments that slowly debilitate populations. This is the argument that Kristen Simmons (2017) develops in her account of the violent policing of Indigenous communities at Standing Rock in the US. Such weaponized atmospheres fit into a broader tradition of warfare designed to "neutralize the enemy" through environmental manipulation. The logic of warfare not only guides direct physical injury to bodies but also underpins processes of modifying the milieu to reproduce and endure relations of violence (see also Funambulist, 2017). These examples show that atmospheres, far from being neutral, are often a register of power that is crucial for sustaining authoritarian regimes and colonial interventions.

This chapter also brought questions of subjectivity to the fore, advancing feminist calls to "think war ... through social and political subjects" (Cowen and Gilbert, 2008: 1). The embodied orientations in the city, such as orientations toward avoiding some areas of the city and frequenting others, involve a process of simultaneously situating oneself in relation to the banality of warfare. The axes of safe/risky, us/them, enemy/ally shape the subjectivities of differently positioned residents. In doing so, race, class, and gender are constantly renegotiated under the conditions of who feels at home or out of place in the city. The way residents occupy space, the way they move in the city, and the kind of habitual actions that they take point to how intersectional identities are constituted atmospherically. The examples in this chapter showed different ways of inhabiting space, as residents were either extending into space or being blocked by space (Ahmed, 2006), shaping racial, classed, and gendered relations. Crucially, in cities of banal warfare, atmospheres operate by differentiating between people whose lives are considered valuable and in need of protection and those people who are deemed as a source of threat and danger, or simply as disposable (Mbembe, 2003). In other words, the atmospheric power is a geopolitical one, as it performatively constitutes subjects and objects of security, danger, and threat. The intertwined relationship between affect and geopolitics (Pain, 2009; Puar, 2009; Laketa, 2016; Gökarıksel and Secor, 2020) is at the heart of these processes. Atmospheres of banal warfare further constitute subjects as anticipated to be dangerous, as opposed to being known to be dangerous. This orientation toward the future is an important aspect of the atmospheres of banal warfare, as has been discussed in terms of urban planning for "the war yet to come" and vigilance and radicalization as anticipatory affective regimes.

To conclude, atmospheres of banal warfare are an effect of reiterative actions, materialized through routinized arrangements of bodies, objects, and spaces that produce war as a category of experience. These atmospheric relations are characterized by increased unease about the future and a taxing sense of alertness in anticipation of danger that slowly envelopes spaces and bodies. Such atmospheric relations authorize distrust, antagonism, boundary making, exclusion, and containment. Unevenly and differentially composed atmospheres additionally cultivate military values and authoritarian and colonial regimes, entrenching racial, gendered, and classed power relations.

FIVE

Affective Unsettling of Urban Warfare

Chapters 2 to 4 focus on the intricate and interconnected set of discourses, urban landscapes, and affectivities that are enrolled in the military logics of control and defense that shape the cities of banal warfare. At the same time, the spaces and practices of undoing geopolitical violence remain underexplored and are often hidden from view (Koopman, 2011; Megoran, 2011; Woon, 2011; Fregonese, 2012; Loyd, 2012). This chapter seeks to draw attention to the ongoing interplay of forces through which urban warfare is undermined and unsettled.

To do so, we turn again to Daniel's dance get-togethers at the Place de la République (discussed in Chapter 4). When we discussed his years-long engagement in organizing dance evenings, Daniel stated that his motivation did not come solely from the love of dancing, but out of "*énervement*" (anger and frustration). He felt that "*toujours on t'empêche*" (he is always prevented from doing things). The city authorities had banned Daniel from putting on the event numerous times—sometimes due to lack of official authorization from the city and sometimes because it was perceived as a security threat or a public health hazard. During the state of emergency from 2015 to 2017, when massive gatherings in public spaces were severely restricted, Daniel joined with a protest movement called Nuit Debout (Up All Night), which started in the spring of 2016 as a form of occupation of the Place de la République to contest the upcoming labor reform law (Loi travail El Khomri) and to challenge the ban on mass demonstrations under the state of emergency. Nuit Debout initiated a wide range of activities on the square, including public debates, information booths on the contested labor law and the state of emergency, and music and art performances as well as the setting up of tents and the sharing of food. The transformation of the square into a place of encampment led to an intense police presence on and around the square, and there were violent clashes between the protesters and the police on several occasions.[1] For Daniel, the movement provided an opportunity to reappropriate the square. He said: "If they have the right to set fires, we have the right to dance." Here, Daniel drew a contrast between the violent tactics of protest and dancing on the square as a rather joyous means of creating spaces of opposition and contestation.

Besides the restrictions on dance evenings during the anti-terrorist state of emergency, further constraints were posed by the health state of emergency in 2020. In August 2020, when Daniel and I talked, the city had already lifted the complete ban on public circulation, but Daniel was still struggling with mandatory mask-wearing while dancing on the square as there were times when municipal authorities closed down the event because participants were not wearing masks appropriately. He felt constantly frustrated, wanting to engage actively and creatively in the city, but he did not give up despite his own economic and social hardship. For Daniel, the dance get-togethers were a way of "living together" ("*pour vivre-ensemble*"). Strangers, friends, and passers-by were welcome to simply dance together, to move their bodies to the rhythm of the music on the square. Dance get-togethers became a way to engage freely in space and with other people and to actively create something in the city, even if this was ephemeral and fleeting.

In contrast to the atmospheric walls and fortifications and the affective atmospheres of enclosure discussed in the previous chapter, we can understand the dance events as a performative tactic to change the mood of the place. It can be seen as a process of staging a different atmosphere, one defying the military logic of vigilance and suspicion. They were a means of disrupting normative bodily orientations and habitual normative ways of feeling in this space, which modified the affective tonality of the place. Here, Daniel's experience of being blocked by space was reshaped into a way of extending into space, creating an atmosphere of shared and embodied vulnerability. If atmospheres are instrumental in supporting and rendering durable conditions of state violence and associated racism, xenophobia, and nationalism, they can also be mobilized to undo violence and transform relations of oppression.

The atmospheres of shared vulnerability can be thought of as an "atmospheric otherwise" (Simmons, 2017), or affective geographies that unsettle and performatively undo the logic of warfare and militarism in the city. Daniel's dance get-togethers on the Place de la République were thus part of everyday spaces and practices of undoing geopolitical violence, ones that were frequently overlooked and ignored but which were vital in constructing plural geographies of peace in the city. While there has certainly been extensive consideration of more publicized and visible protest movements and urban revolts to contest state violence and different forms of state neglect, racism, and patriarchy (such as the Nuit Debout movement, described earlier), this chapter turns next to a consideration of the more mundane, ephemeral, and embodied ways of reconfiguring the notion of cities at war. This centers on affective atmospheres that performatively reshape the relations of power that underpin cities of banal warfare by forming different ambient contours of space. The discussion engages with definitions of peace and antiviolence suggested by feminist scholars and activists (Koopman, 2011; Loyd, 2012; Butler, 2016/2009; Dijkema, 2022). Here, peace is foremost understood as a process. Peace is approached as a performative, contingent, and unfixed unfolding, one that is enabled and constrained through embodied practices. The body plays an important role in this process as the focus on the body literally "makes space for peace" (Koopman, 2011). In her writings on "anti-geopolitics," Sara Koopman states: "I am interested in how geopolitics is thought differently not just by writing about bodies, but by moving bodies" (2011: 277). Affective atmospheres as spatial phenomena address how bodies are aligned and oriented in social spaces; thus, they are a site of potential for moving bodies to attune to others, shaping geographies of interconnectedness, porousness, and mutual interdependencies (Simmons, 2017).

Undoing military urbanism

Militarist urban landscapes play a crucial role in the process of materializing the discourses on urban warfare in everyday spaces, rendering it a durable and pervasive condition. Earlier chapters have looked specifically at the trajectory of deploying the national army to patrol the city streets, with soldiers being gradually replaced by militarized police forces. What was once considered the exception has metamorphosed into the new normal, whereby the logic of emergency has seamlessly transitioned into the process of governing. Together with building different security infrastructures to "design out terrorism," the militarized police are pivotal in shaping atmospheres of warfare within the fabric of everyday city spaces. The rationale behind the related public policies and urban planning agendas is ostensibly rooted in the preservation of order and security, with police and military forces assuming the mantle of primary agents tasked with maintaining peace in urban environments. This state-sponsored waging of wars in cities as a means of ensuring peace is not, however, universally accepted, as shown by the numerous urban actors involved in this study who challenge this approach.

Even police officers, typically positioned as enforcers of such policies, have contributed dissenting voices by challenging the prevailing narrative of militarist peace as the panacea for urban security. One of them, Peter, a Belgian federal police officer working at the anti-terrorist unit, took a critical stand on the new militarist approach to policing. When we met at a coffee shop in central Brussels in the early summer of 2019, we began discussing the changes he had encountered in his work in the city since the last time we spoke, which was in the very aftermath of the attacks and the lockdown in 2016. Similar to other members of the police who took part in this study, he mentioned extensive changes in the equipment and modes of policing in the city. He brought up the issue of the mandatory bulletproof vests carried by police officers as well as the introduction of submachine guns with what he called "a war caliber." He concluded that the police now "carry more equipment than a World War II soldier." "Is this going to bring peace?" he asked, following the question with a short and decisive: "I don't think so." He further mentioned the large investment in security infrastructures, such as bollards and other architectural barriers, as a political move:

> They are putting up barriers since the guy is an enemy ... because they [the politicians] call them the enemy! The enemy is already your enemy, and we don't care about him. What we will do is we dissuade him from coming to us or we [will] disrupt his capacity to come into action. They [the politicians, the government] love it! Because it is more manly, more physical, and the images are better for their voters. And as a policeman, I believe it is not efficient.

Peter referred to the "us versus them" dichotomy that structures political discourses on the "enemy" and has saturated the dominant framing of the indiscriminate killings and attacks in the city. He further highlighted the masculinist vision of strength and state power that these policies seek to promote, as argued in Chapter 3.

When I asked him why he thought these developments were not adequately addressing the issue of so-called "terrorist" violence, he brought up two related issues. On one hand, he considered military equipment to be not only a disproportionate answer to urban violence but also one that actively invokes the framework of warfare, saying: "It is not a kind of gun you use in the city unless you want to start a war." On the other hand, he brought up the issue of the changes in the very embodiment of police officers carrying this equipment. He discussed how the equipment initially made police officers feel empowered and strong, but after a while it started to exacerbate their own feelings of being under threat, as was discussed in the previous chapter. Peter added that the equipment, such as bulletproof vests, also detach the police officer from their surroundings: "it cuts you off from the people." This feeling of externality in relation to the urban environment had been further amplified, according to Peter, because most police officers in Brussels come from other regions in the country, not from the city itself. He said:

> That is my biggest fear when it comes to Brussels. The police officers are starting to look like an occupation army. Because most of the policemen don't come from Brussels; they come from outside of Brussels. So they, kind of, come to bring peace. ... Like the Blue Helmets who come from Denmark and they come to bring peace to places like Somalia ... it starts to look like that.

Here, Peter drew connections between policing in the city and western liberal notions of "peacebuilding" that inform peacekeeping "interventions" as a form of warfare or occupation. His comments further echoed the long-standing critique of humanitarianism that aligns with military values in cities and places across the global south and east (Ben-Ari and Elron, 2001; Fassin and Pandolfi, 2010; Brković, 2016; Li, 2019; Spesny, 2019). This scholarship highlights the ongoing convergence between warfare, humanitarianism, and peacekeeping (for example, through the "blue helmets", the United Nations peacekeeping division) that further perpetuates and consolidates contemporary militarism and geopolitical violence.

Peter and I discussed possible future developments with regard to militarized policing, and in Peter's opinion, the tendency was to gradually intensify this form of policing with the further introduction of military equipment, values, and logic. However, he thought this intensification would occur incrementally, without police officers and members of the public noticing. His comments support this book's argument that warfare in the city is recreated and normalized through affective atmospheres, or modes of embodiment and orientation in the urban environment, that involve subtle and incremental changes in the surroundings. War atmospherics are thus less noticeable as they are assembled in a gradual manner, with warfare and militarism becoming lived and embodied conditions. Peter noted that the process of dismantling war atmospherics also takes shape gradually, at least initially. For him, the undoing of banal warfare involves many seemingly mundane forms of disobedience on the part of police officers, enacted as not consciously formed oppositions. He gave examples of police officers taking off their bulletproof vests on hot days or simply forgetting to put them on at times. With time, according to Peter, police officers might gradually decide to leave their weapons in the station or the chief of police might even suggest placing them in what is called the central station, and so on. Thus, the undoing of military urbanism also works atmospherically, gradually shifting modes of embodiment and incrementally, often unconsciously, destabilizing the notion that "we are at war." Peter thought that, ultimately, when encountering a heavily armed police officer in the city, other police officers might "simply think that he looks ridiculous." In other words, such mundane and rather incoherent shifts in atmospheric relations could slowly denaturalize the notion of warfare and thus undermine its presumed common-sense logic. However, for this form of barely noticeable shift to take place, according to Peter, "it will involve a lot of energy from people like me." Peter was, thus, himself invested in sustaining these forms of mundane disobediences and deviations; for him, it remained a conscious effort to challenge the normative framework of warfare in the city.

Embodiment as a form of conscious resistance to militarized police was also raised in my conversations and walk-alongs with city residents, particularly in relation to violent clashes with the police during public demonstrations. For Adrian, a senior-year high school student who went on a walk-along at the Place de la République in August 2020, the square was primarily a place of public protest. Placed strategically in the geographical heart of Paris, the square is a focal point where numerous protests commence and culminate, making it a symbolic and practical hub for the convergence of diverse voices seeking social and political change. Adrian was living with his family in a neighborhood close to the square, so he had, over the years, observed the growing violence when protest movements were active there. As a teenager, he had started collecting police bullet casings from the city streets as well as other police artifacts as reminders of the mundane presence of violence in the city (as mentioned in Chapter 4, Benoit similarly collected artifacts). Adrian was supportive of the calls to social justice voiced during many of these protests and often went to the Place de la République to express his support. During our walk-along, he showed me the streets surrounding the square where heavily armed police were usually stationed during protests. Their presence heightened, for him, the feeling of exposure to violence. However, he quickly noted that it would be more likely to be subjected to police violence in "*les banlieues*" (the suburbs) of the city than on the Place de la République. Adrian commented that in the suburbs of Paris, the police could act with more impunity, and he mentioned several cases of death at the hands of police officers in these areas, including the much-publicized case of Adama Traoré, who died in 2016 while in police custody in a northern suburb. Traoré's death had sparked a series of protests, and these were reignited in the summer of 2020 when the police officers involved were exonerated from any misconduct. The protests, under the banner of "Justice for Adama," formed part of the global Black Lives Matter movement and stood against the police violence to which Black and Arab communities in France were being subjected. For Adrian, the police on the Place de la République were much more careful regarding the use of violence, primarily, in his opinion, because these incidences were often filmed and documented by the protesters and/or the media. His comments align with critiques of police violence in France that stress their disproportionate effects in the racialized working-class neighborhoods, the so-called *quartiers populaires* (see, for example, Rigouste, 2017; Dijkema, 2022).

Adrian mentioned several tactics for consciously resisting state violence during protests on the square; these aimed to strengthen group solidarity and embodied protection. For example, one of the most important things for Adrian, when he attended protests on the square, was to wear black clothing. "It is important that everybody wears black," he said, so that members of the protest movement can be protected from prosecution by the police. While Adrian said he was not a "*casseur*" (a rioter) himself, he supported such forms of voicing dissent. By wearing black, he could protect individual members of the collective from being targeted by the police. Forming the so-called "black bloc" has been a long-time tactic of protest in France, Belgium, and elsewhere. It enables protesters to remain anonymous and shapes the aesthetic experience of the protest. The wearing of black clothes and/or face coverings is a thus form of staging an atmosphere, one that engenders affective experience of unity and solidarity but also intimidation and strength against militarized police. Rather than an unconscious disruption of the normative embodiments as a mode of shifting relations of military urbanism, as discussed by Peter earlier, this is an example of an intentional and highly visible staging of an atmosphere that seeks to contest state violence.

Building solidarities, challenging gentrification

Chapter 3 considers the way urban warfare takes shape not only through modes of policing but also through economic restructuring and urban redevelopment programs that support economic precarity and processes of gentrification. Geopolitical violence is argued to be further sustained by different economic policies as forms of state neglect. Chapter 3 raises the issue of the processes of gentrification in Molenbeek, which have been gradually excluding the existing residents of that working-class neighborhood, either through the material form of the newly refurbished buildings or by adopting economic policies that do not address those residents' needs. To destabilize processes of gentrification, several initiatives seek to give visibility to the existing residents. One example is the Migration Museum in Molenbeek, which opened in 2019 with the support of regional and municipal government and civil society initiatives in the neighborhood. As their website states: "This museum does not just tell the story of migration in Brussels. It honors the many migrants who have helped to shape Brussels" (foyer.be, nd). Situated near the Canal area of Molenbeek, the museum creates an environment for telling different stories about the neighborhood, sharing oral histories of the guest workers, refugees, EU citizens, and many others engaged in the dynamic and ongoing processes of migration to and from Brussels. The stories are thus a site of struggle over the social meaning of this neighborhood, which dominant discourses describe as either a "wasteland" or a "breeding ground for terrorists" (see Chapter 3). While the dominant depictions are disembodied and dehumanize the residents, the museum's counternarratives affirm humanity through the act of storytelling.

Struggle over the social meaning of the city is not the only struggle initiated with the processes of gentrification and economic restructuring. For many residents, these processes bring about struggle over access to basic needs, such as housing, employment, and affordable healthcare. Navigating the precarious terrain of life in the city is, for many, an ongoing pursuit, coming as an effect of long-term state neglect of marginalized communities in the cities. Social and economic precarity thus often came up as a topic of conversation during walk-alongs and interviews with residents. However, I want to turn now to different practices that challenge the effects of gentrification and precarity, practices I call "atmospheric labor." These are practices in the city that aim to mitigate precarity by modifying affective relations between urban residents. One form of such atmospheric labor was brought up in my conversation with Nao, the head of one of many *maisons de quartier* (community centers) near the Place de la Bourse in the City of Brussels. The main purpose of the community centers, established and financed by the City of Brussels municipal government, is to strengthen social cohesion in the city and offer social support to different groups of marginalized people in the neighborhoods, from unemployed youth and mothers with young children to older people struggling with access to basic services. Nao described her work in one of the centers as *"prendre la colère"* (literally, "taking the anger") from the neighborhood, especially the anger present in the neighborhood following the attacks in 2016 and the anger cause by the ongoing urban redevelopment in the neighborhood, exemplified by the pedestrianization of the Place de la Bourse. This taking of anger is an atmospheric labor that seeks to modify affective relations of anger, turning them into other affective modalities that diffuse or dampen the anger. This is a form of creating peace for the residents of the neighborhood, which has long been labeled as a dangerous, violent, and threatening place. Peace here engenders a normative understanding as an absence of anger; however, there are many other ways of shaping affective geographies of peace, where peace has a plural and non-normative meaning.

Coming back to the Place de la République in Paris, the bustling environment of a public square is not only a place of lively gatherings and public protests; it is also a place of assembly for many people grappling with the harsh reality of their precarious living conditions, including individuals dealing with mental health challenges, substance misuse, enduring unstable housing situations, and precarious employment. Some come to the square to sleep; some come to meet others; some are selling different goods, such as the many food vendors on the square. The square is, in many ways, a microcosm of the broader urban challenges resulting from economic restructuring under late capitalism, state neglect, and gentrification as a process of displacement of working-class residents.

Khalil, a man in his forties, would come to the square almost daily, bringing food and clothing to those in need and occasionally helping those with acute housing needs in the neighborhood. As we walked around the square together on a warm evening in November 2021, many people approached to greet him. He was well known by many different groups present on the square and he cordially exchanged a few words with them. Khalil, a son of Algerian migrants, said that he had grown up in the context of poverty and unemployment in a northern neighborhood in Paris. Substance misuse, mental health problems, and unstable housing have been part of Khalil's life for a long time.

In addressing the question of the so-called "terrorist" violence that has affected this neighborhood, Khalil remarked on the processes of normalization of the notion of warfare that had shaped the contours of daily life in the city, commenting: "We are told (by the government) … that it's a new form of warfare and that we basically have to adapt to it." Challenging this narrative, Khalil highlighted state-induced vulnerabilities and marginalization brought about by socioeconomic precarity and state neglect. As we discussed his engagement in organizing access to basic needs for people on the square, he said: "Why am I doing this? I give myself an activity, an ecological action on my environment that has a positive impact on me." In other words, he saw his daily work of gathering donations and distributing them to those in need as a way to impact the environment and his immediate surroundings; through these actions, he sought to modify the toxic conditions of life he and his fellow citizens have been subjected to. He primarily aimed to resist the affective relation of what he called "indifference." He described indifference as a process of alienation and disinterest in the city, whereby "if you fall on the ground, nobody will pick you up." Therefore, his daily effort to help those in need was not simply physical labor but atmospheric labor as well, labor he described as "recognizing yourself in another person." It is thus a form of affective solidarity that fosters affective relations of interconnectedness and mutual interdependencies. In contrast to the atmospheric labor of "taking the anger," the atmospheric labor of solidarity in Khalil's case is a daily practice of cultivating relationally constituted, non-normative atmospheres of peace, wherein peace has overlapping and competing meanings.

Atmospheric labor of rebuilding a sense of place

In the heart of Molenbeek, a bustling market was in full swing as I walked with Sophie one morning in June 2023. Thursday was the day when Place Communale and the adjacent square, in front of the Saint-Jean-Baptiste parish, transformed into a lively hub, teeming with local vendors, residents, and visitors. The array of stalls, adorned with colorful produce and an eclectic mix of clothes, shoes, household items, and other goods, created a sensory spectacle. Sophie took us around the stalls as, for her, the market encapsulated the essence of her daily life in the neighborhood and she wanted to show the vibrancy of Molenbeek's social life. She enjoyed the social character of the neighborhood, a place where she had lived most of her life. The sounds of the bustling neighborhood made her feel comfortable and safe since, as she said, it was never quiet in the neighborhood and there were always people walking, "even at night." She continued: "there's always an atmosphere [*l'ambiance*]. There are always people. ... That's what I like about the neighborhood." Moreover, the sight of Moroccan clothes and food being sold at the market and on the Chaussée de Gand boulevard made her feel connected to her Moroccan homeland. It also lessened her feelings of isolation and exclusion; as she put it: "I've never felt like a foreigner here ... I've never felt alone." "In other places, other areas of the city, yes, because I wear a headscarf [*le foulard*]." In other words, the headscarf marked Sophie out as a foreigner in other areas of Brussels, echoing Islamophobic discourses of the global war on terror (see also Hancock and Mobillion, 2019; Najib, 2020; Najib and Teeple Hopkins, 2020). For this reason, Sophie felt uncomfortable in other areas of the city and preferred to stay in Molenbeek, where she had a sense of belonging and experienced being at ease.

Away from the hustle and noise of the bustling market, Sophie's friend Véronique took us on a walk-along to a park in Molenbeek, a place she liked because the greenery and tranquil atmosphere made her feel calm and secure. The day of the walk-along, also in in June 2023, had started with some tension for Véronique, as she had spent the morning reading about the events in Paris a few days before. The news was filled with stories about the murder of 17-year-old Nahel Merzouk, shot dead by police in a western suburb of Paris. This young French man of Moroccan and Algerian descent had been shot by a police officer, who was working for La direction de l'ordre public et de la circulation (Public Order and Traffic Department), after failing to comply with a traffic stop. In the years before this, France had recorded an increase in police shootings during traffic stops, with Black and Arab residents often the target. Some scholars connect these shootings with the law adopted in February 2017 as part of a series of legal measures to fight terrorism in the country. Among other things, the law permitted police officers to shoot even when citizens did not represent a serious and immediate threat[2] (Roché et al, 2022; Jabkhiro and Foroudi, 2023).

Following the killing of Nahel, a series of protests, marches, and urban revolts filled the streets in the suburban areas of Paris and other cities in France and Belgium as a call for justice over the killing of the teenager. The connections between the two cities and the feelings of injustice spanning different geographies were palpable in Molenbeek and other areas of Brussels in the days following the murder. Véronique brought up the events surrounding the murder of Nahel when we met in front of her house in Molenbeek. As a mother of three young men, she said she understood the pain and rage of the protesters. She also agreed with them "that something has to be done (regarding police violence)," but she preferred to stay calm, saying "I can't break something because I'm enraged." For Véronique, it was important to talk to people and build connections with them, even in situations where she perceived that others were afraid of her or mistrusted her on account of her wearing "*le foulard*." Véronique had arrived in Brussels over 30 years ago; she came as a young woman from Morocco, leaving her whole family behind. Initially, she had a hard time adapting to her life in Brussels since she did not know many people and did not speak the language. In time, she found her place in the city, and having reached the point where her children were adults, she felt freer to engage actively in the neighborhood. Together with Sophie and several other women in Molenbeek, Véronique had been organizing a host of social and artistic activities in the neighborhood, from parties and dance events to arts and crafts activities, primarily for the local women and children. For both Sophie and Véronique, this engagement was an important way of building a sense of belonging and community in the city and contesting the geographic imaginaries of violence imposed on the place. As Véronique said: "People come here, they think we're fighting a war every day, but in Molenbeek, we're not fighting a war. There are good things going on."

The atmospheric labor of shaping a sense of place mobilizes the notion of peace that erodes and destabilizes urban warfare. This atmospheric labor, moreover, generates geographical counter-imaginaries. During our conversations, Sophie and

Véronique invoked the image of the places that they cultivate together in the city, describing them as "full of colors," "a rainbow," and simply "*trop belle*" (beautiful) places. The atmospheric labor of building a sense of place is, in many ways, at the forefront of gradually shifting affective landscapes of fear and discrimination into spaces of care, peace, and anti-violence.

Atmospheres of urban peace

This chapter underscored the contingency of power relations that underpin the cities of banal warfare. It addressed processes of shifting the affective atmospheres of urban warfare as practices of assembling affective atmospheres of urban peace. The unplanned embodied practices and orientations in the city as well as the atmospheric labor of sustaining communities, solidarities, and building a sense of place do not rest on the agency of a sovereign subject (Butler, 2016/2009); moreover, they contest the notion of peace that informs state-sanctioned peacekeeping "interventions." What these practices do highlight are the relational and affective alliances that shape the plural geographies of peace.

Drawing from scholarship on war-torn cities, the practices of undoing wars in an urban context often rest on mundane and embodied doings that incrementally erode or modify relations of violence. Stories of daily life in war-torn cities reveal countless examples of how simple, everyday acts—like sharing coffee or visiting a neighbor—become powerful forms of cultivating counter-atmospheres to warfare. These routines are not just about surviving; they are embodied affirmations of life and humanity countering the destructive forces that seek to erase them. In Sarajevo during nearly four years of siege, residents hosted concerts, threw parties, cultivated urban gardens, and created spaces of undoing of the relations of warfare (Maček, 2009; Hodžić, 2017). These acts, rooted in community and creativity, are at the time of writing echoed in cities in Ukraine and Gaza, where people continue to carve out humanity in the midst of devastation. These often-mundane acts shift the common portrayals of war, which often reduce cities to anonymous battlegrounds devoid of human life. Through personal stories and testimonies, residents challenge the notion that violence is the natural state of these cities, offering instead a vision of places filled with defiant life (Woodward, 2007). The very act of living performatively reinstantiates the war-torn city, not just as a site of destruction but also as a place where life stubbornly persists. In other moments, feminist and women's peace movements reclaim intimate, domestic spaces, turning homes into sanctuaries amid ever-present violence in the city (Shalhoub-Kevorkian, 2009; Enloe, 2010). In the context of long-term pervasive conflict and chronic violence in post-conflict cities, attention is drawn to collective healing processes that rework intergenerational and spatial trauma by establishing new affective connections to place. It is an iterative, embodied, and autonomous process that Catalina Ortiz and Oscar Gómez Córdoba call "territorial healing," shedding light on "the spatial dimensions of collective healing" (2024: 126).

The chapter further argued that the porous and indeterminate quality of atmospheres widens the possibilities of unsettling and undermining the violent and toxic conditions of urban warfare. These include both mundane and more visible shifts, deviations, and obstructions of violent atmospheric relations. Atmospheres of shared vulnerability and solidarity can be understood as the milieus of connection that are crucial for articulating the demands for social justice. Finally, in Paris and Brussels, atmospheres of warfare and peace exist side by side as an ongoing interplay of forces through which geopolitical violence is established and undermined in the process of enacting plural geographies of peace.

Conclusion: The Urbicidal Geographies of Cities of Banal Warfare

Numerous places across Ukraine and Gaza have become tragic symbols of cities at war, each enduring prolonged and devastating conflict. Cities, enclaves, and camps have faced relentless destruction and witnessed profound human suffering. The widespread destruction, displacement, and trauma that these and other places throughout global urban peripheries endure, are not isolated tragedies. They are not aberrations that are distant and disconnected to "our" lives and "our" cities within the western metropolitan centers. Urban warfare needs to be seen as a global process unevenly shaping geographies of violence and conflict in ways that interconnect seemingly disparate places, including places that are not overtly marked by armed destruction. This book seeks to put into question the comfortable distance in relation to war by thinking *with* war-torn cities. *Cities of Banal Warfare* developed through the process of reversing the gaze, as an embodied standpoint that draws on knowledges and ideas on warfare that are rendered marginal or aberrant. In doing so, it seeks to disrupt the normative (western, colonial) configuration of knowledge about where warfare happens and what urban warfare looks like. In tracing connections and building relational urban geographies, new vocabularies are developed, ones that advance decolonial urbanisms and at the same time open up new avenues of thought on urban processes in metropolitan centers.

One of the lessons learned in the process of reversing the gaze is that warfare is a condition that pervades and infuses everyday, intimate, and affective landscapes of urban life, as opposed to being an exceptional event happening elsewhere. Starting from urbicides and their aftermath in the cities of the Balkans, the book traced urban processes in Paris and Brussels as a form of atmospheric urbicide. Affective atmospheres are a loose and unstable, yet powerful, constellation of discourses, objects, and affectivities through which urbicidal geographies are anchored and strengthened. The processually and performatively assembled atmospheres inaugurate logics of control, fortification, siege, and enclosure, enabling systematic yet diffuse and impalpable annihilation of the urban as a place of encounter and of heterogenous flows. More than a physical destruction, such urbicidal geographies are porous, amorphous, and routinized arrangements of bodies, affects, places, and narratives that solidify warfare as a condition within the material and intimate spaces of the city. The normalized, taken-for-granted, or banal warfare extends across a range of different spatialities, dismantling boundaries between state and private actors, civilian and war spaces, private and public relations. With the ability to collapse existing distinctions, urban warfare transcends disparate contexts, shaping a range of different practices, from urbicidal planning, urban redevelopment, policing, city marketing, and provision of social services to the everyday activities of residents. Moreover, urbicidal geographies extend further into the future. The anticipated future wars, violence, disease, and social collapse are also part of the annihilating processes shaping socio-spatial relations in the present. This is especially evident in the state politics of affect that inaugurates vigilance and radicalization as anticipatory regimes of life in the city. In other words, the potential of what *might* happen is rendered palpable in the present through affective atmospheres.

The attention to the construction of urbicidal geographies across cities in the global east and south has also advanced thinking on warfare through relations of subjectivity. Subjects of danger, threat, safety, and protection are complexly assembled in relation to the banality of warfare. Here, the figures of citizen-soldiers, "could-be" terrorists, sentinels, and enemies within shape subjectivities of differently positioned actors. Such subjectivities antagonize religious, ethnic, racial, and classed differences and enable sectarian geographies. In Paris and Brussels, the associated imaginative geographies of the city at war construct orientalized spaces of violence. The imaginative geographies support nationalist discourses and rely on racialized and colonial ideas on danger and threat. We see here the scaling down of the narrative on the "clash of civilizations" at the level of the urban, where some urban areas are seen as the enemy that threatens "our" social and political order, fueling nationalistic and orientalist discourses on the barbaric and unsanitary "other."

Furthermore, the construction of subjects and objects of banal warfare has a long history rather than being a novel development. While some of my interlocutors narrate their experience of the city through the language of change and shift, describing either forms of "new" military policing and urban governance agendas or shifted habitual activities, this book highlights the long imperial and colonial genealogy underscoring the processes of banal warfare, which have predominantly affected marginalized communities in cities. Systemic discrimination, police violence, and social exclusion have long formed the conditions of life of these communities. Therefore, the attention to affective atmospheres, rather than a shift in socio-spatial relations in the city, is important as it reveals the increased intensity of relations of exclusion, mistrust, and constraint as well as their extended reach deep within everyday places and embodied lives, which contributes to further normalization of war atmospherics.

Finally, positioning war-torn urban peripheries, across the Balkans and the global south, as epistemic sources opens up possibilities for rethinking notions of urban peace and healing processes. Regimes of difference formed in relation to the banality of warfare in the city are never fixed or stable, but rather need to be constantly recreated in everyday life. The inherent instability of atmospheric relations, and the associated subject positions, is also a site of potential for undoing war atmospherics. The wounding and healing processes in cities operate within the same performative framework as routinized arrangements of bodies, objects, and affectivities. The "atmospheric otherwise" is thus always potentially present, unsettling, shifting, and dissolving war atmospherics through relations of interconnectedness and mutual interdependence.

Questions of power are integral to the production and reproduction of atmospheric relations, and here we have begun to gain insight into the ways the power constellations of militarism and othering function atmospherically. Future work is needed to continue to shed light on how imperialism, racism, colonialism, patriarchy, and nationalism, as well as austerity regimes and neoliberal dispossession, function atmospherically, paying attention to how these conditions become settled and normalized in places and bodies. What is more, we still know very little about how atmospheres can be a tool of change in relation to the durable and pervasive oppressive relations. In a world marked by wars, emergencies, and rising social and spatial inequalities, paying attention to atmospheric relations of violence and difference is even more pressing.

Notes

one Reversing the Gaze, Rethinking Urban Conflict

1. On the notion of performativity and space, see Butler (2015), Gregson and Rose (2000), and Laketa (2018); on performativity and affective atmospheres, see Bille and Simonsen (2021).

two Urban Warfare: From State of Emergency to Lockdown

1. Parts of this chapter were previously published in an article: S. Laketa and S. Fregonese (2023). Lockdown and the intimate: Entanglements of terror, virus, and militarism. *Environment and Planning C: Politics and Space*, *41*(8), 1521–1535. https://doi.org/10.1177/2399654422 1143041

three Everyday Urban Landscapes as Battlescapes

1. Interview in November 2019.
2. Interview with a police officer, anti-terrorist unit, Brussels, June 2016.
3. Interview with members of Bruxelles Prévention et Sécurité/Brussel Preventie en Veiligheid and the Brussels Office for Urban Planning Perspective, June 2019.
4. Interview with a police officer, situational prevention unit, Paris, January 2020.
5. Interview with a police officer, situational prevention unit, Paris, January 2020.
6. For further discussion of the transfer of knowledge from Israeli military and private security companies in urban and security planning in western cities, see Graham (2011).
7. Interview with a police officer, public order and traffic unit, Paris, January 2020.
8. Interview in June 2023.

four Affective Atmospheres "on the Front Line"

1. Interview in October 2021.
2. For further discussion on emotions, police work, and the construction of the city as a space of war, see Pauschinger (2020).

3. Interview in August 2020; for more information on the "yellow vest" protests, see Kipfer (2019).
4. Interview with a high-ranking police officer, Prefecture de Police, January 2020.
5. Interview in January 2020.
6. For further discussion on the police genealogies in an international setting, besides the French police (Rigouste, 2021), see Neocleous (2014).
7. Interview with a high-ranking police officer, anti-terrorist unit, Brussels, June 2019.
8. Interview in January 2020.
9. Interview in December 2021.
10. Walk-along in September 2020.
11. Walk-along in June 2023.
12. Interview in June 2019.
13. For more on the discursive framing of radicalization in Belgium, see Figoureux and Van Gorp (2020).
14. Interview in June 2019.
15. Interview in June 2019.
16. For further discussion on affective atmospheres of the war on terror and Muslim subjectivities, see Zarabadi (2020).

five Affective Unsettling of Urban Warfare

1. For more information on the protest movement, see Kokoreff (2016); for a discussion on counter-atmospherics created by the Nuit Debout movement, see Fregonese and Laketa (2022); for a discussion on how atmospheres are used in policing protest crowds, see Wall (2019).
2. They could shoot when citizens were *likely* to harm themselves or others when fleeing from a traffic stop.

References

Abujidi, N. (2014). *Urbicide in Palestine: Spaces of Oppression and Resilience*. Abingdon: Routledge.

ACAT France (Action des chrétiens pour l'abolition de la torture) (2020). *Maintien de l'ordre: à quel prix?* ACAT. www.acatfrance.fr/public/r_mo_web-pp.pdf

Adey, P., Brayer, L., Masson, D., Murphy, P., Simpson, P., and Tixier, N. (2013). "Pour votre tranquillité": Ambiance, atmosphere, and surveillance. *Geoforum*, *49*, 299–309. https://doi.org/10.1016/j.geoforum.2013.04.028

Ahmed, S. (2004a). Affective economies. *Social Text*, *22*(2), 117–139.

Ahmed, S. (2004b). *The Cultural Politics of Emotion*. Edinburgh: Edinburgh University Press.

Ahmed, S. (2006). *Queer Phenomenology: Orientations, Objects, Others*. Durham, NC: Duke University Press.

Aijazi, O. (2024). *Atmospheric Violence: Disaster and Repair in Kashmir*. Philadelphia: University of Pennsylvania Press.

Alloul, J. (2019). Can the "Muhajir" speak? European Syria fighters and the digital un/making of home. In N. Fadil, M. de Koning, and F. Ragazzi (Eds) *Radicalization in Belgium and the Netherlands: Critical Perspectives on Violence and Security* (pp 217–245). London: I.B. Tauris.

Alves, J. A. (2021). Fatal blow: Urbicidal geographies, pax colonial and black sovereignty in the Colombian city. *Environment and Planning D: Society and Space*, *39*(6), 1055–1072. https://doi.org/10.1177/02637758211042022

Amnesty International (2017). Europe: Dangerously Disproportionate: The Ever-Expanding National Security State in Europe. London: Amnesty International. www.amnesty.org/en/documents/eur01/5342/2017/en/

Amnesty International (2018a). *"War of Annihilation"*: Devastating Toll on Civilians, Raqqa – Syria. London: Amnesty International. www.amnesty.org/en/documents/mde24/8367/2018/en/

Amnesty International (2018b). Punished without Trial: The Use of Administrative Control Measures in the Context of Counter-Terrorism in France. London: Amnesty International. www.amnesty.org/en/documents/eur21/9349/2018/en/

Amnesty International (2020, May 6). FRANCE: Pratiques policières pendant le confinement: Amnesty International dénonce des cas de violations des droits humains (press release). www.amnesty.fr/presse/des-usages-de-la-force-illegaux-pendant-le-confinement

Amoore, L. (2007). Vigilant visualities: The watchful politics of the war on terror. *Security Dialogue*, *38*(2), 215–232. https://doi.org/10.1177/0967010607078526

Amoore, L. (2009). Algorithmic war: Everyday geographies of the war on terror. *Antipode*, *41*(1), 49–69. https://doi.org/10.1111/j.1467-8330.2008.00655.x

Anderson, B. (2009). Affective atmospheres. *Emotion, Space and Society*, *2*(2), 77–81. https://doi.org/10.1016/j.emospa.2009.08.005

Anderson, B. (2017). Cultural geography 1: Intensities and forms of power. *Progress in Human Geography*, *41*(4), 501–511. https://doi.org/10.1177/0309132516649491

Appadurai, A. (2006). *Fear of Small Numbers: An Essay on the Geography of Anger*. Durham, NC: Duke University Press.

Arfsten, K.-S. (2019). Before, now, and after the event of terror: Situational terror awareness for civilians in US Homeland Security. *European Journal for Security Research*, *5*, 223–258. https://doi.org/10.1007/s41125-019-00054-9

Azzouz, A. (2023). *Domicide: Architecture, War and the Destruction of Home in Syria*. London: Bloomsbury Publishing.

Bakić-Hayden, M. (1995). Nesting orientalisms: The case of former Yugoslavia. *Slavic Review*, *54*(4), 917–931. https://doi.org/10.2307/2501399

Barabantseva, E., Mhurchú, A. N., and Peterson, V. S. (2021). Introduction: Engaging geopolitics through the lens of the intimate. *Geopolitics*, *26*(2), 343–356. https://doi.org/10.1080/14650045.2019.1636558

REFERENCES

Belcher, O. (2018). Anatomy of a village razing: Counterinsurgency, violence, and securing the intimate in Afghanistan. *Political Geography*, *62*, 94–105. https://doi.org/10.1016/j.polgeo.2017.10.006

Ben-Ari, E., and Elron, E. (2001). Blue Helmets and White Armor: Multi-nationalism and multi-culturalism among UN peacekeeping forces. *City & Society*, *13*(2), 271–302. https://doi.org/10.1525/city.2001.13.2.271

Bénézit, J. (2022, February 4). « On porte encore l'uniforme comme une carapace »: des policiers veulent « libérer la parole » sur les cas de suicides. *Le Monde*. www.lemonde.fr/societe/article/2022/02/04/on-porte-encore-l-uniforme-comme-une-carapace-comment-des-policiers-veulent-liberer-la-parole-sur-le-mal-etre-dans-leurs-rangs_6112318_3224.html

Benjamin, W. (2023/1983). *Charles Baudelaire: A Lyric Poet in the Era of High Capitalism*. London: Verso.

Berlant, L. (1998). Intimacy: A special issue. *Critical Inquiry*, *24*(2), 281–288. https://doi.org/10.1086/448875

Berlant, L. (2011). *Cruel Optimism*. Durham, NC: Duke University Press.

Bhan, G. (2019). Notes on a Southern urban practice. *Environment and Urbanization*, *31*(2), 639–654. https://doi.org/10.1177/0956247818815792

Bhattacharyya, G. (2013). *Dangerous Brown Men: Exploiting Sex, Violence and Feminism in the "War on Terror."* London: Zed Books.

Bille, M., and Simonsen, K. (2021). Atmospheric practices: On affecting and being affected. *Space and Culture*, *24*(2), 295–309. https://doi.org/10.1177/1206331218819711

Billig, M. (2010/1995). *Banal Nationalism*. Los Angeles: Sage.

Bjelić, D. I., and Savić, O. (Eds) (2002). *Balkan as Metaphor: Between Globalization and Fragmentation*. Cambridge, MA: MIT Press.

Blagojević, M. (2009). *Knowledge Production at the Semiperiphery: A Gender Perspective*. Belgrade: Institut za kriminološka i sociološka istraživanja.

Blanchard, E. (2018). Legs et leçons de la guerre d'Algérie. *Plein droit*, *117*(2), 12–15. https://doi.org/10.3917/pld.117.0012

Boatca, M. (2006). Semiperipheries in the world-system: Reflecting Eastern European and Latin American experiences. *Journal of World-Systems Research*, *12*(2), 321–346. https://doi.org/10.5195/jwsr.2006.362

Böhme, G. (2017). *Atmospheric Architectures: The Aesthetics of Felt Spaces*. London: Bloomsbury Academic.

Bou Akar, H. (2018). *For the War Yet to Come: Planning Beirut's Frontiers*. Stanford, CA: Stanford University Press.

Boulakia, T., and Mariot, N. (2023). *L'attestation. Une expérience d'obéissance de masse, printemps 2020*. Paris: Éditions Anamosa.

Bravvo (Service de prévention de la Ville de Bruxelles) (nd). Qu'est-ce que la radicalisation violente? https://bravvo.bruxelles.be/quest-ce-que-la-radicalisation-violente

Brković, Č. (2016). Scaling humanitarianism: Humanitarian actions in a Bosnian town. *Ethnos*, *81*(1), 99–124. https://doi.org/10.1080/00141844.2014.912246

Butler, J. (2015). *Notes Toward a Performative Theory of Assembly*. Cambridge, MA: Harvard University Press.

Butler, J. (2016/2009). *Frames of War: When Is Life Grievable?* London: Verso.

Canal.Brussels (nd). Histoire. https://canal.brussels/fr/territoire/histoire

Carabelli, G. (2018). *The Divided City and the Grassroots: The (Un)making of Ethnic Divisions in Mostar*. Singapore: Palgrave Macmillan.

Césaire, A. (2014). *Discours sur le colonialisme: Suivi du Petit matin d'Aimé Césaire*. Paris: République des Lettres.

Chadwick, R. (2021). On the politics of discomfort. *Feminist Theory*, *22*(4), 556–574. https://doi.org/10.1177/1464700120987379

Coaffee, J. (2004). Rings of steel, rings of concrete and rings of confidence: Designing out terrorism in central London pre and post September 11th. *International Journal of Urban and Regional Research*, *28*(1), 201–211. https://doi.org/10.1111/j.0309-1317.2004.00511.x

Coaffee, J. (2021). *The War on Terror and the Normalisation of Urban Security*. Abingdon: Routledge.

REFERENCES

Cohen, R. (1995, March 12). FILM; A Balkan gyre of war, spinning onto film. *The New York Times.* www.nytimes.com/1995/03/12/movies/film-a-balkan-gyre-of-war-spinning-onto-film.html

Colls, R. (2012). Feminism, bodily difference and non-representational geographies. *Transactions of the Institute of British Geographers, 37*(3), 430–445. https://doi org/10.1111/j.1475-5661.2011.00477.x

Coward, M. (2009). *Urbicide: The Politics of Urban Destruction.* Abingdon: Routledge.

Cowen, D., and Gilbert, E. (2008). *War, Citizenship, Territory.* Abingdon: Routledge.

Cusicanqui, S. R. (2012). Ch'ixinakax utxiwa: A reflection on the practices and discourses of decolonization. *South Atlantic Quarterly, 111*(1), 95–109. https://doi.org/10.1215/00382876-1472612

De Backer, M., and Melgaço, L. (2021). "Everybody has to move, you can't stand still": Policing of vulnerable urban populations during the COVID-19 pandemic in Brussels. In R. van Melik, P. Filion, and B. Doucet (Eds) Global *Volume 3: Public Space and Mobility,* Reflections on COVID-19 and Urban Inequalities (pp 47–54). Bristol: Bristol University Press.

Degen, M. M., and Rose, G. (2012). The sensory experiencing of urban design: The role of walking and perceptual memory. *Urban Studies, 49*(15), 3271–3287. https://doi.org/10.1177/0042098012440463

Diaz, I. I., and Mountz, A. (2020). Intensifying fissures: Geopolitics, nationalism, militarism, and the US response to the novel coronavirus. *Geopolitics, 25*(5), 1037–1044. https://doi.org/10.1080/14650045.2020.1789804

Dijkema, C. (2022). Creating space for agonism: Making room for subalternised voices in peace research. *Conflict, Security & Development, 22*(5), 475–494. https://doi.org/10.1080/14678802.2022.2122697

Dikeç, M. (2011). *Badlands of the Republic: Space, Politics and Urban Policy.* New York: John Wiley & Sons.

Dikeç, M. (2013). Immigrants, *banlieues,* and dangerous things: Ideology as an aesthetic affair. *Antipode, 45*(1), 23–42. https://doi.org/10.1111/j.1467-8330.2012.00999.x

Dixon, D. P., and Marston, S. A. (2011). Introduction: Feminist engagements with geopolitics. *Gender, Place & Culture*, *18*(4), 445–453. https://doi.org/10.1080/0966369X.2011.583401

Dowler, L., and Sharp, J. (2001). A feminist geopolitics? *Space and Polity*, *5*(3), 165–176. https://doi.org/10.1080/13562570120104382

Dowling, R., Lloyd, K., and Suchet-Pearson, S. (2017). Qualitative methods II: "More-than-human" methodologies and/in praxis. *Progress in Human Geography*, *41*(6), 823–831. https://doi.org/10.1177/0309132516664439

Duru, A. (2019). "A walk down the shore": A visual geography of ordinary violence in Istanbul. *Environment and Planning D: Society and Space*, *37*(6), 1064–1080. https://doi.org/10.1177/0263775819859362

Enloe, C. H. (2010). *Nimo's War, Emma's War: Making Feminist Sense of the Iraq War*. Berkeley: University of California Press.

Fadil, N., Ragazzi, F., and de Koning, M. (2019). *Radicalization in Belgium and The Netherlands: Critical Perspectives on Violence and Security*. London: I.B. Tauis.

Fall, J. J. (2020). Fenced in. *Environment and Planning C: Politics and Space*, *38*(5), 771–794. https://doi.org/10.1177/2399654420933900

Fanon, F. (2008). *Black Skin, White Masks* (trans R. Philcox, revised edition). New York: Grove Press.

Fassin, D. (2011). *La force de l'ordre*. Paris: Seuil.

Fassin, D., and Pandolfi, M. (2010). *Contemporary States of Emergency: The Politics of Military and Humanitarian Interventions*. New York: Zone Books.

Faure, E. (1982). *Mémoires I. Avoir toujours raison … C'est un grand tort*. Paris: Plon.

Fawaz, M. (2009). Neoliberal urbanity and the right to the city: A view from Beirut's periphery. *Development and Change*, *40*(5), 827–852. https://doi.org/10.1111/j.1467-7660.2009.01585.x

Fawaz, M., Harb, M., and Gharbieh, A. (2012). Living Beirut's security zones: An investigation of the modalities and practice of urban security. *City & Society*, *24*(2), 173–195. https://doi.org/10.1111/j.1548-744X.2012.01074.x

REFERENCES

Figoureux, M., and Van Gorp, B. (2020). The framing of radicalisation in the Belgian societal debate: A contagious threat or youthful naivety? *Critical Studies on Terrorism*, *13*(2), 237–257. https://doi.org/10.1080/17539153.2020.1714415

Fontaine, J. (2022). When girls walk: Mobilities of and resistance to affective atmospheres of unwelcome. *Space and Culture*, *25*(4), 633–644. https://doi.org/10.1177/1206331220985459

Foucault, M. (1977). *Discipline and Punish: The Birth of the Prison* (trans A. Sheridan). New York: Pantheon.

Foyer.be (nd). MigratieMuseumMigration. www.foyer.be/migratiemuseummigration/?lang=en

France 24 (2015, November 16). Paris attack probe turns to Belgium's "Islamist pit stop" of Molenbeek. www.france24.com/en/20151116-belgium-molenbeek-paris-attacks-islamist-investigation

Fregonese, S. (2012). Urban geopolitics 8 Years on: Hybrid sovereignties, the everyday, and geographies of peace. *Geography Compass*, *6*(5), 290–303. https://doi.org/10.1111/j.1749-8198.2012.00485.x

Fregonese, S. (2019). *War and the City: Urban Geopolitics in Lebanon*. London: I.B. Taurus.

Fregonese, S., and Laketa, S. (2022). Urban atmospheres of terror. *Political Geography*, *96*, art 102569. https://doi.org/10.1016/j.polgeo.2021.102569

Funambulist magazine (2017). Issue: Toxic Atmospheres, issue 14. https://thefunambulist.net/magazine/14-toxic-atmospheres

Gandy, M. (2017). Urban atmospheres. *Cultural Geographies*, *24*(3), 353–374. https://doi.org/10.1177/1474474017712995

Gatti, A. (2019). Urban terrorist sanctuaries in Europe: The case of Molenbeek. In S. Pektas and J. Leman (Eds) *Militant Jihadism: Today and Tomorrow* (pp 151–176). Leuven: Leuven University Press.

Genç, F. (2021). Governing the contested city: Geographies of displacement in Diyarbakır, Turkey. *Antipode*, *53*(6), 1682–1703. https://doi.org/10.1111/anti.12753

Ghalbzouri, M. E. (2018). Etre un jeune de Molenbeek après les attentats de Paris et de Bruxelles. *Centre Bruxellois d'Action Interculturelle*, *340*.

Gökarıksel, B., and Secor, A. J. (2020). Affective geopolitics: Anxiety, pain, and ethics in the encounter with Syrian refugees in Turkey. *Environment and Planning C: Politics and Space*, *38*(7–8), 1237–1255. https://doi.org/10.1177/2399654418814257

Graham, S. (2006). Cities and the "war on terror." *International Journal of Urban and Regional Research*, *30*(2), 255–276. https://doi.org/10.1111/j.1468-2427.2006.00665.x

Graham, S. (2008). *Cities, War, and Terrorism: Towards an Urban Geopolitics*. New York: John Wiley & Sons.

Graham, S. (2011). *Cities Under Siege: The New Military Urbanism*. London: Verso Books.

Gregory, D. (2004). *The Colonial Present: Afghanistan. Palestine. Iraq.* Maldem, MA: Blackwell.

Gregson, N., and Rose, G. (2000). Taking Butler elsewhere: Performativities, spatialities and subjectivities. *Environment and Planning D: Society and Space*, *18*(4), 433–452. https://doi.org/10.1068/d232

Gusic, I. (2019). *Contesting Peace in the Postwar City: Belfast, Mitrovica and Mostar.* Cham: Springer.

Hammami, R. (2019). Destabilizing mastery and the machine: Palestinian agency and gendered embodiment at Israeli military checkpoints. *Current Anthropology*, *60*(S19), S87–S97. https://doi.org/10.1086/699906

Hancock, C., and Mobillion, V. (2019). "I want to tell them, I'm just wearing a veil, not carrying a gun!" Muslim women negotiating borders in femonationalist Paris. *Political Geography*, *69*(1), 1–9. https://doi.org/10.1016/j.polgeo.2018.11.007

Harvey, D. (2005). The political economy of public space. In S. Low and N. Smith (Eds) *The Politics of Public Space* (pp 17–34). London: Routledge.

Heath-Kelly, C. (2017). The geography of pre-criminal space: Epidemiological imaginations of radicalisation risk in the UK Prevent Strategy, 2007–2017. *Critical Studies on Terrorism*, *10*(2), 297–319. https://doi.org/10.1080/17539153.2017.1327141

REFERENCES

Hergon, F. (2021). The state of emergency at home: House arrests, house searches, and intimacies in France. *Conflict and Society*, 7(1), 42–59. https://doi.org/10.3167/arcs.2021.070104

Hodžić, T. (Director) (2017). *Scream for Me Sarajevo* [Film]. Prime Time.

Howell, A. (2018). Forget "militarization": Race, disability and the "martial politics" of the police and of the university. *International Feminist Journal of Politics*, 20(2), 117–136. https://doi.org/10.1080/14616742.2018.1447310

Human Rights Watch (2016a, February 3). France: Abuses under state of emergency. www.hrw.org/news/2016/02/03/france-abuses-under-state-of-emergency

Human Rights Watch (2016b, November 3). Grounds for concern: Belgium's counterterror responses to the Paris and Brussels attacks. www.hrw.org/report/2016/11/03/grounds-concern/belgiums-counterterror-responses-paris-and-brussels-attacks

IBSA – L'Institut Bruxellois de Statistique et d'Analyse (nd). Molenbeek-Saint-Jean. https://ibsa.brussels/chiffres/chiffres-cles-par-commune/molenbeek-saint-jeanr

Jabkhiro, J. and Foroudi, L. (2023, July 3). France riots: What are rules on police shooting at traffic stops? *REUTERS*. www.reuters.com/world/europe/french-police-use-of-force-powers-road-traffic-stops-2023-06-28/

Jambon, J. (2015, November 14). Jan Jambon in VTM Nieuws: "Ik ga Molenbeek opkuisen." www.janjambon.be/nieuws/jan-jambon-in-vtm-nieuws-ik-ga-molenbeek-opkuisen?pq=nieuws/archief/2015&page=0#views-row-5

Jaminé, S., and Fadil, N. (2019). (De-)radicalization as a negotiated practice: An ethnographic case study in Flanders. In N. Fadil, F. Ragazzi, and M. de Koning (Eds) *Radicalization in Belgium and The Netherlands: Critical Perspectives on Violence and Security* (pp 169–193). London: I.B. Taurus.

Jansen, S. (2015). *Yearnings in the Meantime: "Normal Lives" and the State in a Sarajevo Apartment Complex*. New York: Berghahn Books.

Jarry, E. (2017, October 3). Five detained over wired explosives found in posh Paris neighbourhood. *Reuters*. www.reuters.com/article/uk-france-security-minister-idUKKCN1C80HT

Kadich, D. (2021). Young people, hip-hop, and the making of a "grammar for unpolitics" in Sarajevo, Bosnia and Herzegovina. *Geopolitics*, *26*(5), 1307–1330. https://doi.org/10.1080/14650045.2019.1608436

Kaldor, M. (1999). *New and Old Wars: Organised Violence in a Global Era*. Stanford, CA: Stanford University Press.

Kaldor, M., and Sassen, S. (Eds) (2020). *Cities at War: Global Insecurity and Urban Resistance*. New York: Columbia University Press. https://doi.org/10.7312/kald18538-013

Kaplan, R. D. (1993). *Balkan Ghosts: A Journey through History*. New York: St. Martin's Press.

Katz, C. (2007). Banal terrorism: Spatial fetishism and everyday insecurity. In D. Gregory and A. Pred (Eds) *Violent Geographies: Fear, Terror, and Political Violence* (pp 349–361). New York: Routledge.

Khayyat, M. (2022). *A Landscape of War: Ecologies of Resistance and Survival in South Lebanon*. Oakland: University of California Press.

Khiari, S. (2009). *La contre-révolution coloniale en France: De Gaulle à Sarkozy*. Paris: Fabrique.

Kipfer, S. (2019). What colour is your vest? Reflections on the yellow vest movement in France. *Studies in Political Economy*, *100*(3), 209–231. https://doi.org/10.1080/07078552.2019.1682780

Kipfer, S., and Goonewardena, K. (2007). Colonization and the new imperialism: On the meaning of urbicide today. *Theory & Event*, *10*(2). https://doi.org/10.1353/tae.2007.0064

Kokoreff, M. (2016). Nuit debout sur place: Petite ethnographie micropolitique. *Les Temps Modernes*, *691*(5), 157–176. https://doi.org/10.3917/ltm.691.0157

Koopman, S. (2011). Alter-geopolitics: Other securities are happening. *Geoforum*, *42*(3), 274–284. https://doi.org/10.1016/j.geoforum.2011.01.007

Krasmann, S., and Hentschel, C. (2019). "Situational awareness": Rethinking security in times of urban terrorism. *Security Dialogue*, *50*(2), 181–197. https://doi.org/10.1177/0967010618819598

REFERENCES

Kundnani, A. (2014). *The Muslims Are Coming! Islamophobia, Extremism, and the Domestic War on Terror.* London: Verso.

Kusenbach, M. (2003). Street phenomenology: The go-along as ethnographic research tool. *Ethnography*, *4*(3), 455–485. https://doi.org/10.1177/146613810343007r

Kušić, K., Lottholz, P., and Manolova, P. (2019). From dialogue to practice: Pathways towards decoloniality in Southeast Europe. Special issue on Decolonial Theory & Practice in Southeast Europe. *dВЕРСИЯ*. https://dversia.net/4644/dversia-decolonial-theory-practice-southeast-europe/r

La Défense (nd). Notre mission Vigilant Guardian. www.mil.be/fr/nos-missions/belgique-operation-vigilant-guardian#debriefing

Laketa, S. (2016). Geopolitics of affect and emotions in a post-conflict city. *Geopolitics*, *21*(3), 661–685. https://doi.org/10.1080/14650045.2016.1141765

Laketa, S. (2018). Between "this" side and "that" side: On performativity, youth identities and "sticky" spaces. *Environment and Planning D: Society and Space*, *36*(1), 178–196. https://doi.org/10.1177/0263775817723632

Laketa, S. (2024). War-torn cities: Making feminist sense of urban warfare. In L. Peake, A. Datta, and G. Adeniyi-Ogunyankin (Eds) *Handbook on Gender and Cities* (pp 75–84). Cheltenham: Edward Elgar Publishing. https://doi.org/10.4337/9781786436139.00014

Laketa, S., and Fregonese, S. (2023). Lockdown and the intimate: Entanglements of terror, virus, and militarism. *Environment and Planning C: Politics and Space*, *41*(8), 1521–1535. https://doi.org/10.1177/23996544221143041

Lasoen, K. L. (2017). Indications and warning in Belgium: Brussels is not Delphi. *Journal of Strategic Studies*, *40*(7), 927–962.

Le Monde (2013, February 15). Pour Valls, pas de loi sur le non-cumul des mandats avant 2016. www.lemonde.fr/politique/article/2013/02/15/manuel-valls-craint-plusieurs-merah-en-france_1833116_823448.html

Le Monde (2019, April 12). Les suicides dans la police atteignent un niveau « hors norme » en 2019. www.lemonde.fr/police-justice/article/2019/04/12/suicides-de-policiers-un-chiffre-hors-norme-depuis-le-debut-de-l-annee_5449581_1653578.html

Li, D. (2019). *The Universal Enemy: Jihad, Empire, and the Challenge of Solidarity*. Stanford, CA: Stanford University Press.

Loyd, J. M. (2009). "A microscopic insurgent": Militarization, health, and critical geographies of violence. *Annals of the Association of American Geographers*, *99*(5), 863–873. https://doi.org/10.1080/00045600903253478

Loyd, J. M. (2012). Geographies of peace and antiviolence. *Geography Compass*, *6*(8), 477–489. https://doi.org/10.1111/j.1749-8198.2012.00502.x

Maček, I. (2009). *Sarajevo Under Siege Anthropology in Wartime*. Philadelphia: University of Pennsylvania Press.

Makaš, E. (2007). Representing Competing Identities: Building and Rebuilding in Mostar, Bosnia and Herzegovina. PhD Thesis.

Malmström, M. F. (2019). *The Streets Are Talking to Me: Affective Fragments in Sisi's Egypt*. Oakland: University of California Press.

Mbembe, A. (2003). Necropolitics. *Public Culture*, *15*(1), 11–40. https://doi.org/10.1215/08992363-15-1-11

McKittrick, K. (2011). On plantations, prisons, and a black sense of place. *Social & Cultural Geography*, *12*(8), 947–963. https://doi.org/10.1080/14649365.2011.624280

Mechaï, H., and Hergon, F. (2020). "Make yourself at home!": The French state of emergency and home searches in 2015–2017. *The Funambulist*, *29*, 38–43.

Meeus, B., Van Heur, B., and Arnaut, K. (2019). Migration and the infrastructural politics of urban arrival. In B. Meeus, K. Arnaut, and B. Van Heur (Eds) *Arrival Infrastructures* (pp 1–32). Cham: Palgrave Macmillan. https://doi.org/10.1007/978-3-319-91167-0_1

Megoran, N. (2011). War *and* peace? An agenda for peace research and practice in geography. *Political Geography*, *30*(4), 178–189. https://doi.org/10.1016/j.polgeo.2010.12.003

REFERENCES

Miller, J. C., and Laketa, S. (2019). The "magic of the mall" revisited: Malls and the embodied politics of life. *Progress in Human Geography*, *43*(5), 910–926. https://doi.org/10.1177/0309132518794274

Ministère des Armées (nd). Opération SENTINELLE. www.defense.gouv.fr/operations/territoire-national/france-metropolitaine/operation-sentinelle

Mitchell, T. (1991). *Colonising Egypt*. Berkeley: University of California Press.

Mitropoulos, A. (2020, February 13). Against quarantine. *The New Inquiry*. https://thenewinquiry.com/against-quarantine/

Moderbacher, C. (2020). "Nothing is expensive, everything cheap, nothing explosive!" Side stories from Molenbeek, Brussels. *Migration and Society*, *3*(1), 287–293. https://doi.org/10.3167/arms.2020.030127

Morin, K. M. (2013). "Security here is not safe": Violence, punishment, and space in the contemporary US penitentiary. *Environment and Planning D: Society and Space*, *31*(3), 381–399. https://doi.org/10.1068/d15011

Najib, K. (2020). Spaces of Islamophobia and spaces of inequality in Greater Paris. *Environment and Planning C: Politics and Space*, *39*(3), 606–625. https://doi.org/10.1177/2399654420941520

Najib, K., and Teeple Hopkins, C. (2020). Geographies of Islamophobia. *Social & Cultural Geography*, *21*(4), 449–457. https://doi.org/10.1080/14649365.2019.1705993

National Counter Terrorism Security Office (2022). Evacuation, invacuation, lockdown, protected spaces. www.protectuk.police.uk/evacuation-invacuation-lockdown-protected-spaces

Neocleous, M. (2014). *War Power, Police Power*. Edinburgh: Edinburgh University Press.

Nguyen, N. (2019). *Suspect Communities: Anti-Muslim Racism and the Domestic War on Terror*. Minneapolis: University of Minnesota Press.

Ochs, J. (2011). *Security and Suspicion: An Ethnography of Everyday Life in Israel*. Philadelphia: University of Pennsylvania Press.

Ortiz, C. (2023). Storytelling otherwise: Decolonising storytelling in planning. *Planning Theory*, *22*(2), 177–200. https://doi.org/10.1177/14730952221115875

Ortiz, C., and Gómez Córdoba, O. (2024). Territorial healing: A spatial spiral weaving transformative reparation. *Planning Theory*, *23*(2), 110–130. https://doi.org/10.1177/14730952231181129

Pain, R. (2009). Globalized fear? Towards an emotional geopolitics. *Progress in Human Geography*, *33*(4), 466–486. https://doi.org/10.1177/0309132508104994

Pain, R. (2015). Intimate war. *Political Geography*, *44*, 64–73. https://doi.org/10.1016/j.polgeo.2014.09.011

Parnell, S., and Oldfield, S. (2014). *The Routledge Handbook on Cities of the Global South* (Vol 2014). London: Routledge.

Pauschinger, D. (2020). Working at the edge: Police, emotions and space in Rio de Janeiro. *Environment and Planning D: Society and Space*, *38*(3), 510–527. https://doi.org/10.1177/0263775819882711

Perspective.Brussels (2018). *Guide à l'intégration de dispositifs de sécurité dans l'espace public: Région de Bruxelles-Capitale*. https://perspective.brussels/sites/default/files/documents/bbp_guidesecu_fr_v06.pdf

Perspective.Brussels (nd). Territoire du Canal. https://perspective.brussels/fr/projets/perimetres-dintervention/territoire-du-canal

Police Watch (2020). Rapport Police Watch: Abus policiers et confinement. https://policewatch.be/files/Rapport-Police-Watch-LDH-2020.pdf

Ponsaers, P., and Devroe, E. (2017). The Brussels bombings – striking a balance between law enforcement and risk management. In A. M. Kellner (Ed) *Democracy and Terrorism – Experiences in Coping with Terror Attacks: Case Studies from Belgium, France, Israel and Norway* (pp 5–14). Berlin: Friedrich-Ebert Stiftung.

Puar, J. K. (2009). Prognosis time: Towards a geopolitics of affect, debility and capacity. *Women & Performance: A Journal of Feminist Theory*, *19*(2), 161–172. https://doi.org/10.1080/07407700903034147

Puar, J. K. (2018/2007). *Terrorist Assemblages: Homonationalism in Queer Times*. Durham, NC: Duke University Press.

REFERENCES

Pullan, W. (2011). Frontier urbanism: The periphery at the centre of contested cities. *The Journal of Architecture*, *16*(1), 15–35. https://doi.org/10.1080/13602365.2011.546999

Rabie, K. (2021). *Palestine Is Throwing a Party and the Whole World Is Invited: Capital and State Building in the West Bank*. Durham, NC: Duke University Press.

Ramadan, A. (2009). Destroying Nahr el-Bared: Sovereignty and urbicide in the space of exception. *Political Geography*, *28*(3), 153–163. https://doi.org/10.1016/j.polgeo.2009.02.004

Ren, J. (2022). A more global urban studies, besides empirical variation. *Urban Studies*, *59*(8), 1741–1748. https://doi.org/10.1177/00420980221085113

Rigouste, M. (2009). *L'ennemi intérieur: La généalogie coloniale et militaire de l'ordre sécuritaire dans la France contemporaine*. Paris: La Découverte.

Rigouste, M. (2017). From Algeria to the banlieues: A colonial genealogy of the French police. *The Funambulist*, *8*. https://thefunambulist.net/magazine/08-police/podcast-transcripts-algeria-banlieues-colonial-genealogy-french-police-mathieu-rigouste

Rigouste, M. (2021). *La domination policière*. Paris: La fabrique éditions.

Robinson, J. (2016). Comparative urbanism: New geographies and cultures of theorizing the urban. *International Journal of Urban and Regional Research*, *40*(1), 187–199. https://doi.org/10.1111/1468-2427.12273

Robinson, J. (2022). *Comparative Urbanism: Tactics for Global Urban Studies*. Hoboken, NJ: John Wiley & Sons.

Roché, S., le Derff, P., and Varaine, S. (2022, September). Homicides policiers et refus d'obtempérer: La loi a-t-elle rendu les policiers irresponsables? *Esprit*. https://esprit.presse.fr/actualites/sebastian-roche-et-paul-le-derff-et-simon-varaine/homicides-policiers-et-refus-d-obtemperer-44252

Rose, G., Degen, M., and Basdas, B. (2010). More on "big things": Building events and feelings. *Transactions of the Institute of British Geographers*, *35*(3), 334–349. https://doi.org/10.1111/j.1475-5661.2010.00388.x

Ross, K. (2000). Rimbaud and the transformation of social space. *Yale French Studies*, *97*, 36–54. https://doi.org/10.2307/2903213

Rousseau, D. (2006). L'état d'urgence, un état vide de droit(s). *Revue Projet*, *291*(2), 19–26. https://doi.org/10.3917/pro.291.0019

Roy, A. (2009). The 21st-century metropolis: New geographies of theory. *Regional Studies*, *43*(6), 819–830. https://doi.org/10.1080/00343400701809665

Roy, A. (2016). Who's afraid of postcolonial theory? *International Journal of Urban and Regional Research*, *40*(1), 200–209. https://doi.org/10.1111/1468-2427.12274

Said, E. W. (1979). *Orientalism*. New York: Vintage.

Said, E. W. (1994). Travelling theory reconsidered. In *Travelling Theory Reconsidered* (pp 251–268). Stanford, CA: Stanford University Press.

Shalhoub-Kevorkian, N. (2009). *Militarization and Violence Against Women in Conflict Zones in the Middle East: A Palestinian Case-Study*. Cambridge: Cambridge University Press.

Shalhoub-Kevorkian, N. (2017). The occupation of the senses: The prosthetic and aesthetic of state terror. *British Journal of Criminology*, *57*(6), 1279–1300.

Simmons, K. (2017, November 20). Settler atmospherics. *Society for Cultural Anthropology*. https://culanth.org/fieldsights/settler-atmospherics

Smith, S., Neubert, C., Hawkins, M., and Gokariksel, B. (2021). *Feminist Geography Unbound: Discomfort, Bodies, and Prefigured Futures*. Morgantown: West Virginia University Press.

Spesny, S. L. (2019). Urban warfare. In *The Wiley Blackwell Encyclopedia of Urban and Regional Studies* (e-book; pp 1–7). Hoboken, NJ: Wiley Blackwell. https://doi.org/10.1002/9781118568446.eurs0403

Stewart, K. (2011). Atmospheric attunements. *Environment and Planning D: Society and Space*, *29*(3), 445–453. https://doi.org/10.1068/d9109

Sudbury, J. (Ed) (2005). *Global Lockdown: Race, Gender and the Prison-Industrial Complex*. New York: Routledge.

REFERENCES

Sumartojo, S., and Pink, S. (2018). *Atmospheres and the Experiential World: Theory and Methods* (e-book). London: Routledge. https://doi.org/10.4324/9781315281254

Thénault, S. (2007). L'état d'urgence (1955–2005). De l'Algérie coloniale à la France contemporaine: Destin d'une loi. *Le Mouvement Social*, *218*(1), art 63. https://doi.org/10.3917/lms.218.0063

Torrekens, C. (2009). *L'islam à Bruxelles*. Editions de l'Université de Bruxelles.

United Nations Institute for Training and Research (2017). Damage density of Ar Raqqa, Ar Raqqa Governorate, Syria. https://unosat.org/products/1192

van der Saag, E. (2023). *Situated Accounts from within a Stigmatized Area: An Ethnographic Study on Local Views and Experiences Relating to Urban Developments in Molenbeek, Brussels*. Thesis, KTH, Urban and Regional Studies. https://urn.kb.se/resolve?urn=urn:nbn:se:kth:diva-340748

Visit.Brussels (2022, February 24). The canal, an industrial district reborn as a trendy and sustainable neighbourhood. www.visit.brussels/en/visitors/plan-your-trip/the-canal-an-industrial-district-reborn-as-a-trendy-and-sustainable-neighbourhood

Voeten, T. (2015, November 21). Molenbeek broke my heart. *POLITICO*. www.politico.eu/article/molenbeek-broke-my-heart-radicalization-suburb-brussels-gentrification/

von der Burg, L., and Krasmann, S. (2023). Naming the city: On the governing forces of narratives in the formation of security dispositifs. *Critical Studies on Security*, *12*(1), 33–47. https://doi.org/10.1080/21624887.2023.2286770

Wall, I. (2019). Policing atmospheres: Crowds, protest and "atmotechnics." *Theory, Culture & Society*, *36*(4), 143–162. https://doi.org/10.1177/0263276419829200

Weizman, E. (2007). *Hollow Land: Israel's Architecture of Occupation*. London: Verso.

Wetherell, M. (2013). Feeling rules, atmospheres and affective practice: Some reflections on the analysis of emotional episodes. In *Privilege, Agency and Affect* (e-book; pp 221–239). Basingstoke: Palgrave Macmillan. https://doi.org/10.1057/9781137292636_13

Williams, A., Hinck, K., Karklis, L., Schaul, K., and Stamm, S. (2016, April 1). *How two Brussels neighborhoods became "a breeding ground" for terror*. Washington Post. www.washingtonpost.com/graphics/world/brussels-molenbeek-demographics/

Woodward, R. (2007). Narratives of destruction and survival: Writing and reading about life in urban war zones. *Theory & Event, 10*(2). https://muse.jhu.edu/pub/1/article/218096

Woon, C. Y. (2011). Undoing violence, unbounding precarity: Beyond the frames of terror in the Philippines. *Geoforum, 42*(3), 285–296. https://doi.org/10.1016/j.geoforum.2011.04.003

Yacobi, H. (2009). Towards urban geopolitics. *Geopolitics, 14*(3), 576–581. https://doi.org/10.1080/14650040802694091

Yiftachel, O. (1998). Planning and social control: Exploring the dark side. *Journal of Planning Literature, 12*(4), 395–406. https://doi.org/10.1177/088541229801200401

Yiftachel, O. (2020). From displacement to displaceability. *City, 24*(1–2), 151–165. https://doi.org/10.1080/13604813.2020.1739933

Younis, T. (2021). The psychologisation of counter-extremism: Unpacking PREVENT. *Race & Class, 62*(3), 37–60. https://doi.org/10.1177/0306396820951055

Zarabadi, S. (2020). Post-threat pedagogies: A micro-materialist phantomatic feeling within classrooms in post-terrorist times. In B. P. Dernikos, N. Lesko, S. D. McCall, and A. D. Niccolini (Eds) *Mapping the Affective Turn in Education: Theory, Research, and Pedagogies* (pp 69–83). Routledge. https://doi.org/10.4324/9781003004219-8

Zemmour, E. and Farge, L. (2015, November 17). Attentats à Paris: "François Hollande craint de prononcer le nom de notre adversaire", lance Éric Zemmour. *RTL*. www.rtl.fr/actu/debats-societe/attentats-a-paris-francois-hollande-craint-de-prononcer-le-nom-de-notre-adversaire-lance-eric-zemmour-7780537994

Index

References to figures appear in *italic* type.

A

ACAT France 30–31
Adrian (Paris citizen) 91–92
affective atmospheres
 atmospheric labor 94, 95–97, 98–99
 atmospheric otherwise 16, 86–87, 104
 conceptual framework 12–15
 "enemy within" discourse 77–80, 82–83, 103
 police, militarization influences 65–67, 87–92
 racialization, countering initiatives 73–77
 urban peace 99–100
 vigilance, state-cultivated 62–65, 67–72
Ahmed, Sara 77
Algeria 25
Amnesty International 31
anti-ramming devices 47–48, *48–49*, 88

B

Balkan region 4–5, 11–12, 99
banal warfare, conceptualization 2, 16
Beirut 51
Belgium 3, 31
Benna, Zyed 25
Benoit (police officer) 65–66
Billig, Michael 16
Bogdanović, Bogdan 4, 5
bollards 47–48, *48*, 88
Bou Akar, Hiba 51
Brussels
 citizen vigilance 70–71
 colonial legacies 3
 counterterrorist security, political aims 38–40, *39*
 COVID-19, racialized threat 35–36
 de-radicalization initiative 75–76
 lockdowns, terrorism linked 2015/16 27–28
 military policing, internal dissent 87–91
 Operation Vigilant Guardian 29
 Plan Canal 42, 43–44, 54–58, 59–60
 post-attacks "rebrand" 74–75
Brussels Office for Urban Planning Perspective 47
Bruxelles Prévention et Sécurité 47

C

Césaire, Aimé 8
Chirac, Jacques 25–26
Claude (police officer) 68
Collomb, Gérard 33
counterterrorist security
 citizen vigilance, personal stories 68–72
 citizen vigilance, police attitudes 67–68
 "enemy within," symbolic protection 42, 59
 Molenbeek residents' fears 44–45, 57, 60
 perceived threat absurdities 45–46
 Plan Vigipirate 63
 political motivations 38–40, *39*
 psychological adaptations 64–65
 soldiers' visibility as performative 40–42

COVID-19 pandemic 33–36, 79
Coward, Martin 5

D

Daniel (Paris citizen) 77–80, 84–85
de-radicalization programs, Brussels 73–77
deathscapes 1–2, 4

E

Egypt 81–82
Emma (Brussels citizen) 70–71
"enemy within" discourse
 countersecurity, symbolic 42, 59
 de-radicalization initiative, Brussels 73–74
 othering problems 80, 82–83, 103
 police violence 91–92
 public emergencies 77, 78
 racialization and threat fears 77–80
 urban warfare 30
Eric (Paris citizen) 68–69

F

Faure, Edgar 25
France
 anti-terrorism laws 2017 32–33, 97
 colonial legacies 3, 25
 COVID-19 lockdowns 35, 77, 79
 Plan Vigipirate 63, 67–68
 public order, nonlethal weapons use 32
 Raqqa urbicide 31
 state of emergency, laws/implementation 24–27
 state of emergency, militarist framing 26–27, 29–30, 31
Fregonese, Sara 6, 38, 46

G

Gaza 1, 99–100, 101
Geens, Koen 27

Gómez Córdoba, Oscar 100
Graham, Stephen 7, 26

H

Haussmann, Baron 50
Heidi (Molenbeek resident) 44–45
Hollande, François 27, 29–30

I

Ifeta (city official) 73–75
Iris (city official) 76
Islamic State 28–29, 31
Ismail (police officer) 67
Israel 52, 68, 81

J

Jambon, Jan 43–44

K

Kaldor, Mary 6
Katz, Cindy 16, 40–41
Khalil (Paris citizen) 94–96
Khayyat, Munira 9–10
Koopman, Sara 87

L

lockdown measures
 controlled mobility/interactions 29–30
 counterterrorism, UK adoption 34
 COVID-19, military logics applied 33, 34–35
 racialized risks and discourses 35–36
 state enclosure/fortification 34–35
 terrorist linked, Brussels 2015/16 27–28, 33–34
Lucas (city official) 75, 76

M

Macron, Emmanuel 33
Marco (police officer) 61–62, 63–64, 68

INDEX

Mbembe, Achille 44
McKittrick, Katherine 11–12
Merzouk, Nahel 97–98
militarism 15–16
military urbanism
  "boomerang effect" 8
  civilians, conscious resistance 91–92
  military policing, internal dissent 87–91
  police services, France 61–68, 91–92
  securitization 7–8, 87
  vigilance, citizens' embodiment 68–72
Molenbeek municipality, Brussels
  gentrification and exclusion 55–58
  gentrification, destabilization 93–94
  Migration Museum 93
  non-residents' threat fears 70, 71, 72
  Plan Canal 43–44, 54–58
  residents' racial dehumanization 42–43, 54–55, 56, 73–74
  security presence, civilian fears 44–45, 57
  sense of place, rebuilding 96–97, 98–99
  terrorist linked 27, 42, 43, 73
Mostar 4, 11–12

N

Nao (community worker) 94
National Counter Terrorism Security Office, UK 34
New Caledonia 25
Nuit Debout 84–85, 86

O

occupation, violence of 81–82
Office for Urbanism 47
Operation Inherent Resolve 31
Opération Sentinelle 27, 40, 63

Operation Vigilant Guardian 29, 40
Ortiz, Catalina 100

P

Palestine 81
Paris
  citizen vigilance 68–69
  colonial legacies 3
  COVID-19, racialized threat 35–36
  police services,' permanent warfare impacts 61–67
  post-2005 riots, state's 'othering' 25–26
  public spaces, security infrastructures 50–51, 52–53
Paris, 2015 attacks
  "enemy within" discourse 30
  police, consequential vigilance 61–65
  state's militarist response 26–27, 29, 30–31
peace, geographies of 86–87, 94, 99–100
Peter (police officer) 87–91
Place de la Bourse, Brussels 18, 48, 70, 94
Place de la Republique, Paris
  anti-geopolitical activities 84–86, 91–92
  community relief activities 94–96
  public emergency impacts 77–79, 78
  symbolic significance 17–18
Plan Canal, Brussels
  counterterrorist discourse 42–44
  redevelopment, gentrification and exclusion 54–58, 59–60
Plan Vigipirate 63, 67–68
police services
  citizen vigilance, attitudes on 67–68
  civilians, detachment issues 88–90
  demonstrations as acts of war 65–67
  mental health issues 64, 66
  militarization, conscious undoing 90–91
  military weaponry 61, 65, 67, 88

post-2015, heightened vigilance impacts 61–65
racialized shootings 97
public space as defensive space
  future threat/war, planning focus 51–54, 58–59
  Haussmann schemes 50
  Paris, event enclosure/mobility 52–53
  Paris's situational prevention 50–51
  security infrastructures 47–49, *48–49*, 88

R

Raqqa, Syria 31
research, aims/methodology 16–20
Rigouste, Matthieu 67

S

Said, Edward 8–10, 26
Sarkozy, Nicolas 26
sectarian geographies 57, 60, 102–103
Shalhoub-Kevorkian, Nadera 81
Simmons, Kristen 82
Sisi, Abdel Fattah 81–82
situational awareness 64–65
Sophie (Molenbeek resident) 96–97, 98–99
Spinoza, Baruch 13
state of emergency, France
  authorization and powers 24–25, 29–30, 32
  COVID-19 lockdowns 33, 35, 77, 79
  disruptive contestation 84–85
  law origins 24, 25
  Paris 2005 riots, consequential 'othering' 25–26
  Paris attacks 2015, military deployment 26–27, 29, 30–31

T

territorial healing 100
Traoré, Adama 91–92
Traoré, Bouna 25

U

Ukraine 1, 99–100, 101
urban governance
  colonialist logic and racial dehumanization 42, 43–45
  lockdowns' military logics 27–28, 29–30, 34–35
  public emergencies, militarist framing 23, 24–27, 29–30 32–33, 36–37
  war atmospherics 81–83
urban peripheries 7–8, 8–12, 103–104
urban planning
  defensive space focus 51–54
  redevelopment, gentrification and exclusion 54–58, 59–60
  sectarian geographies 57
urban warfare
  anti-geopolitical embodiments 84–87, 99–100, 104
  civilians as "collateral damage" 45
  contemporary strategies 1–2, 101
  demonstrations as acts of war 65–67
  "enemy within" discourse 30
  geographies of peace 86–87, 94, 99–100
  performativity of 58–60
  racialized risks and discourses 36, 42, 95–96, 102–103
  scholarly debates and reframing 5–7
  urban peripheries, decolonizing narratives 8–11
  vigilance, state-cultivated 62–65
urbicide
  definition 4
  geopolitical violence and affects 11–12, 101–102
  place annihilation, Balkans 5
  scholarly debates 5–7

V

Véronique (Molenbeek resident) 97, 98–99

INDEX

vigilance, state-cultivated
  citizens' enrolment, police attitudes 67–68
  citizens' personal embodiment 68–72
  Plan Vigipirate, France 63, 67–68
  police services, permanent warfare impacts 62–65, 97–98

W

walkalongs 18–20
war atmospherics 81–83, 103–104

Z

Zemmour, Éric 43

www.ingramcontent.com/pod-product-compliance
Lightning Source LLC
Chambersburg PA
CBHW071716020426
42333CB00017B/2291